Edith Evans

A Personal Memoir

Edith Evans

A Personal Memoir

by
Jean Batters

Hart-Davis MacGibbon London

Granada Publishing Limited
First published in Great Britain 1977 by Hart-Davis, MacGibbon Ltd
Frogmore, St Albans, Hertfordshire AL2 2NF and
3 Upper James Street, London W1R 4BP

ISBN 0 246 10994 7
Printed in Great Britain by
Butler & Tanner Ltd
Frome and London

Acknowledgements

For permission to reproduce copyright material grateful thanks are due to: Chapman and Hall (extract from James Agate's *The Contemporary Theatre*); the late Mr T. C. Worsley (extracts from *The Fugitive Art*); Sir Harold Hobson (extracts from *Theatre 2* and *The Theatre Now*); Hutchinson Publishing Group (extracts from Sir Beverley Baxter's *First Nights and Footlights* and from Dame Irene Vanburgh's *To Tell My Story*); W. H. Allen & Co. Ltd (extract from Charles Castle's *Noel* and from *Margaret Rutherford*, an autobiography as told to Gwen Robyns); Times Newspapers Ltd (extracts from theatre reviews in *The Times*); and the *Observer* (extract from Sir John Gielgud's appreciation of Dame Edith Evans).

Note

I should make it clear that although I knew Dame Edith for twenty-five years, I never addressed her as Edith. When I was her secretary she said 'it would be bad for discipline', and when eventually she suggested I call her Edith, the Dame Edith habit was too firmly established. But among any of her friends, who later became my friends, I always called her Edith, and that is how I think of her. And that is how I write of her. Pages of Dame Edith, or worse, Dame Edith Evans, is a daunting prospect.

Chapter One

It was in the early 1920s that I first heard the name Edith Evans; the locale was a narrow country road in the Conway Valley in North Wales.

My sister and I had gone down to the station to meet my father – we always called him Robert – on his return from one of his frequent visits to London, where he stayed at his club and took the girl friend of the moment to see his favourite actresses; these included Binnie Hale and Gladys Cooper. But on this particular evening as the car approached our home Gell-y-Forwyn, which we were told meant variously The Maiden's Bower or The House on the Dung Heap, he was raving over a new actress. 'She's not pretty,' he said, 'but she's absolutely marvellous. The most marvellous actress I've ever seen. Her name is Edith Evans.' He must have seen Edith playing Millamant in *The Way of the World* at the Lyric Theatre, Hammersmith, where at that time she was the talk of the town.

It was to be eight years before Edith Evans was more than a name to me, and over twenty years before I became her secretary. By that time Robert was in the last stages of Parkinson's Disease and could not fully appreciate my good fortune.

Although we were living in Wales when I first heard Edith's name, we were not Welsh, but owned a colliery called the Point of Ayr. My grandfather took it over as a gamble in the 1880s, and the miners drew his carriage through the village, hailing him as their saviour. Since then the colliery had prospered, but soon after the

7

First World War it was decided to give up the London office and Robert and his brother Walter moved with their families to Wales.

At that time I was still at school, but on leaving I found life in the country exceedingly dull. Having been to a private school I had no skills or training, but as we knew E. J. Marshall of Marshall and Snelgrove, then a highly aristocratic establishment, it was arranged that I should go there as a hairdressing apprentice. I had no interest in hair, but it seemed a good excuse for living in London, so a room was found for me in the firm's hostel in Bulstrode Street. It was a happy time. I had friends; there were parties; we went to the theatre not, I regret to say, to see Edith Evans, but Fred and Adele Astaire and Jack Buchanan and Elsie Randolph. It was the heyday of revue and musical comedy and none of us would have crossed the street to see a straight play.

After a while, when my money was exhausted, I returned home and spent several years playing games of all kinds, including badminton which I played for North Wales. But eventually this too became dull, particularly meeting the same people year after year, and following Robert's example I went up to London more and more frequently, graduating from musical comedy to straight plays. There were far more matinées then than now, and I usually managed to see two plays a day. In 1932 one of these plays was *Evensong* starring Edith Evans, and the following year it was Edith Evans again, this time playing Gwenny in *The Late Christopher Bean*. Like Robert, I had found my favourite actress.

I was now definitely stage-struck and decided to give up games and find a job in the theatre. Not as an actress: I had an intermittent stammer which might stay away for months and then return at an inconvenient moment, but I had from time to time tried my hand at writing; I could become a playwright.

But where to live? I bought the London evening papers, looking for a cheap room, but before I could settle into some bug-infested attic I was fortunate enough to meet Pat Bell, a woman who lived at the Three Arts Club in the Marylebone Road. This club, famous in its day for such members as Binnie Hale, Gwen Ffrangcon-Davies, and Dodie Smith, had been founded by Lena Ashwell (Lady Simson), whom I was to meet years later when she tried to interest Edith in both spiritualism and Moral Rearmament, without success.

The club was a unique institution, offering reasonable accommodation to women connected with the three arts of music, painting and the theatre. The accommodation was so reasonable that when my future friend Phyllis Morris joined in 1916, a cubicle cost fifteen shillings (75p) a week including all meals, and a good bedroom twenty-seven shillings and sixpence a week (£1.37). I started in a minute slip of a room where I hammered away at my play. No one could have been more amateurish; had the play been produced it would have run for half an hour, and though I possessed a typewriter I had never heard of carbon paper. When I needed, or thought I needed, an extra copy, I typed it separately.

As time passed I did less and less writing and more and more sitting in the lounge and gossiping. Although I did not know it at the time, the great days of the club were over, but being as naïve as I was amateurish I thought that the members I met, many of them elderly, were important in the theatre, particularly as I gathered they had been appearing quite lately. But this 'quite lately' proved to be in 1932 in the crowd scenes of Noël Coward's *Cavalcade*, of which he wrote: 'Most of the cast had been engaged before we left London, and on our return we dealt with the crowd auditions. This was a depressing business. We needed about four hundred, and over a thousand applied.'

My naïvety also led me to buy that splendid publication *Who's Who in the Theatre*, expecting to learn more of my new friends, and was puzzled to find that the only one mentioned was Phyllis Morris.

When I first met Phyl she was playing in *Music in the Air*, an enchanting musical play starring Mary Ellis. Why we became friends I have no idea. Forty years later Phyl said it was because I did not make the best of myself and she wanted to do something about my clothes which she said were pathetically provincial. This I strongly deny, but be that as it may, Phyl and I became friends, for which much thanks; if it were not for her I would never have graduated to being Edith's secretary, but first I was to be Dodie Smith's secretary, and that was Phyl's doing. She and Dodie were life-long friends, having first met at RADA, and now in the 1930s Dodie was the most successful playwright in the country, having written *Autumn Crocus*, *Service*, and *Touch Wood*, and was about to have an even greater success with *Call It a Day* which ran for 509 performances at the Globe Theatre. At this time she was looking for a theatrically-minded secretary as the ones she had had knew nothing of the theatre and cared less. It was Phyl who suggested that I should take a secretarial course and fill the gap. The

It sounded a splendid idea, a case of being of the theatre if not actually in it, so I enrolled at the Triangle Secretarial College in South Molton Street. I was not a star pupil, my only achievement being to have a story accepted by Blackie's Children's Annual. But I learnt to touch-type, which included learning about carbon paper, and I attained an unremarkable speed in something called Speed-writing, considered simpler than shorthand for the not-so-young.

When I had learnt as much as I was capable of learning, I reported to Dodie at Rossmore Court, close to Regent's Park. I was terrified. I knew I was not an efficient secretary, and this state of nerves re-sulted in my spending most of that first day in the lavatory. But by the end of the week I had settled down and stayed with Dodie and Alec (then her manager, later her husband) until the start of the Second World War.

They were infinitely patient, and it was lucky for me that they were my first employers; I should not have lasted a week with any-one less humane than Dodie. But my enthusiasm for the theatre must have compensated for the sheets of ruined notepaper which found their way into the wastepaper basket as I learnt my job at Dodie's expense.

It was with her encouragement that I became a Gallery First Nighter, and it was from the gallery that I saw Edith play Agatha Payne in *The Old Ladies*, the Nurse in *Romeo and Juliet*, Irina Arcadina in *The Seagull*, Rosalind in *As You Like It*, and everything else that she played, including Sanchia Carson in *Robert's Wife*.

But I was not allowed to enjoy Edith without a certain amount of good-natured badinage from Dodie and Alec. Edith was by no means their favourite actress, and they were constantly citing a play called *Tiger Cats* in which she had starred in 1924, and in which her performance had caused them acute embarrassment.

But it had not embarrassed James Agate, then Drama Critic of the *Sunday Times*, a critic not renowned for pulling his punches. He had written:

Can any other actress so act with every line and curve of her body? To suggest the claws of the tigress and the caged, restless walk was obvious and easy. To crouch upon the sofa as you may see her prototype hug a branch in Regent's Park, was equally child's play. But to make us conscious, as we were made conscious, of the fruition in one single human being of millions of years of rapacity in pre-existent states of reptile, bird, fish, mammal, without rasping accent or accentuated leer – this could have been the achievement of none but a very great artist. Miss Evans has every physical advantage for the part. She is, Heaven be praised, plain in the same sense that you might call the Mona Lisa plain; to look upon her is to know the dwindling quality of mere prettiness. I should call her voice glorious, if it were not that I want that word for her intelligence.

Reading that again in the 1970s I can understand how Dodie and Alec felt; I might have felt the same. The fact was that Edith, like any great practitioner in any art, aroused strong passions. Whilst James Agate might call her voice 'glorious' to others it might sound the ultimate discord. People either raved over her or against her. She was a gift to impersonators, and I heard Florence Desmond impersonate her at the London Palladium in the early years of the war. At the age of eighty-six she was still being impersonated.

But my verbal skirmishes with Dodie and Alec were all part of the fun of first nights, and I owe a deep debt of gratitude to Dodie for sending me off to the gallery.

It is not only first nights for which I have to thank her, she taught me a great deal about the theatre, all of which was of value when I became Edith's secretary.

I went on prior-to-London tours, the first of these being *Bonnet over the Windmill* in 1937. I had my first chance of sitting in on rehearsals, again these were of *Bonnet*, and I learnt from Alec how to cope with Dodie's flowers and telegrams after a first night.

The first night of *Dear Octopus* in 1938 was a memorable occasion. It started in deepest gloom as war was expected at any moment, but in the first interval the news broke that Neville Chamberlain was flying to Munich and the gloom changed to blazing floodlights of delight. Dame Irene Vanbrugh described the occasion in her autobiography *To Tell My Story*:

It was the first night of *Dear Octopus* by Dodie Smith. Marie Tempest still holding her own as London's favourite was at the head of the cast. Rumours that day had been busier than ever with shouting on all sides that war with Germany was imminent. The audience as they sat there seemed strained, focusing with difficulty on the imaginary situations of the play. Was there any possibility of peace after all or were we all to be thrown into the cataclysm of agony and

11

battle? Suddenly in the interval, between acts one and two, the news flashed round the theatre. 'Chamberlain is flying to Munich tonight to see Hitler.' It reacted on everyone, galvanizing life, cutting through the heavy clouds of depression.

It is all very well to blame us now, but when one has expected to be blown sky-high, it is only human to be thankful for a reprieve.

After *Dear Octopus* was safely launched, Dodie and Alec sailed for New York, first persuading me to sleep in Alec's flat so that Pongo (the original of Pongo in *The Hundred and One Dalmatians*) should have company. I had no love of large dogs; they scared me, and Pongo knew it, playing up accordingly. As soon as I was in the bathroom he would leap from his basket on to the bed, from where he had to be coaxed with relays of chocolates bought for this purpose from Clare's in Park Road. But by the morning he was back on the bed, growling ferociously if I moved my feet.

Some time before Dodie's return her housekeeper came up from the country for the day and, unlike me, adoring Pongo, offered to take him home with her. I was overjoyed. Life without Pongo was wonderful. But when Dodie returned her first words were: 'Where's Pongo?' and her eyes were alight with anticipation. But when I replied: 'Bertha took him down to the country', the light was extinguished, abruptly and completely. Dodie never reproached me, and it is only now that I fully appreciate her bitter disappointment at being welcomed, not by Pongo, but by me.

When Dodie and Alec again went to America they stayed for years, taking Pongo and their housekeeper with them. Left alone I tidied up the two flats and handed them over to Claude Graham White, the aviator, then the owner of Rossmore Court. I still carried on with Dodie's correspondence from the flat in Kent Terrace which I shared with Phyl Morris, but as war was now inevitable we joined the Auxiliary Fire Service, and on 1 September 1939, we closed our front door and moved to our Fire Station in Devonshire Close, Devonshire Street.

Phyl soon reopened the front door, she was not cut out for a Firewoman but did much good work touring the mining villages with Dame Sybil Thorndike and Sir Lewis Casson. I saw the war out from various Fire Stations in London and the South of England, my only link with the theatre being when I saw Edith in whatever play she might be doing.

12

But at last the war ended, and as soon as I was free from the Fire Service my thoughts returned to playwriting. I had never given up hope that one day I might write a produceable play, and as Dodie was a great encourager of would-be playwrights I had gone on trying, despite the fact that two plays written while I was working for her were both rejected. But now I decided to have a final try. If I failed I could always return to secretarial work – in the theatre, of course.

With my war gratuity I took a furnished flat in George Street, wrote the play, sent it to Elsie Beyer, at that time H. M. Tennent's General Manager, and sat back and waited. After a considerable delay the play was returned. After this it shuttled back and forth a number of times, finally coming to rest in the office of a Repertory Company, in Guildford I think, from which it never returned.

So it was to be secretarial work, but with whom? I sat down and wrote to the three actresses I admired most – Edith Evans, Diana Wynyard, and Flora Robson. Edith was the only one to reply. She telephoned when I was out, and it was several days before I plucked up courage to ring her back. When I did she told me that her secretary was on holiday and would I come to Albany and take some letters? I would. It was 31 July 1946.

Chapter Two

I already knew something of Albany through G. B. Stern, the novelist, who lived there, and whom I met in Tunbridge Wells during the war. She invited me to tea, and some days later I was sitting with her on a bench in her sister's garden burbling about how much I enjoyed her novels, which was true, but blotting my copy book when I concluded by saying: 'One of my favourites is *Who Would Have Daughters?*' Smilingly, and without rancour, Miss Stern informed me that particular book had been written by her friend Marguerite Steen.

But I could not have made too bad an impression as, when the war ended, Miss Stern wrote suggesting that I might care to be her secretary. I nearly accepted but decided that my speedwriting was inadequate for a novelist, and anyhow my true love was the theatre.

Later, when I was finally installed as Edith's secretary, I would meet Miss Stern in the rope walk (the covered way linking the Piccadilly entrance to Albany with Vigo Street) where she promenaded daily, and daily she looked straight ahead, ignoring my presence. I thought, or rather I was sure, that she was piqued that I had preferred Edith to herself.

Dressing to go down to Albany to meet Edith for the first time, I wore not a provincial outfit, but a grey flannel suit and blue pill-box-style hat, both from Lilian Lawler, Dodie's pre-war dressmaker in South Molton Street. Any good clothes we possessed in 1946 were pre-war, as at that time clothes were rationed and needed coupons, of which we never had enough.

Unlike my first day with Dodie, I have no recollection of feeling nervous as I took the bus to Piccadilly. I must have gained a degree of assurance over the years and now, with time to spare, took a stroll round Fortnum and Mason.

Crossing the road from Fortnum's I approached Albany across the courtyard and up the steps to the porter's lodge, presided over by Mercer, the splendid ex-guardsman Head Porter in brown tail-coat and top hat. If I was overawed I need not have been, I was soon to discover that Mercer, and indeed all the Albany porters, were kind, helpful, and unfailingly jolly.

Mercer directed me to the rope walk, on either side of which were the blocks of chambers lettered B to L. I was looking for L block where Edith lived in L 4, and was delighted to find it opposite B 4, the London home of that fictitious character John Worthing. How appropriate that the most famous of Lady Bracknells should live within Wagnerian hailing distance of her nephew.

As I climbed the stone stairs to L 4, I could hear Edith's voice, and as I rang the bell she opened the door wearing a brown and white checked Molyneux suit, with a white nylon blouse tied in a bow at the neck. For me the meeting was entirely satisfactory, well up to expectations; Edith looked and sounded as she did on the stage, her voice had the same authority, almost the same volume, every syllable enunciated.

I was anxious to take in every detail of the scene but Edith was never one for loitering. However, as I followed her through the hall, I did notice a bronze head on a pedestal which, though bearing only a fleeting resemblance to Edith, was extremely pleasing; later I learned that it had been modelled by Dora Gordine. I already knew the sitting-room, it had been featured in a glossy magazine with Edith sitting on a low chair beside the fireplace doing some 'pro-perty' mending. The mantelpiece was cluttered with photographs among which I noticed one of an elderly man and woman sitting on a bench. The woman was obviously Ellen Terry. Later I learned that it was Edith's mother.

It was now time for my speedwriting, rusty and probably more halting than ever, to be put to the test, but although Edith rattled along at breakneck speed it stood the test. This was because most of the letters concerned *Antony and Cleopatra* the play then in re-hearsal, with Edith playing Cleopatra to Godfrey Tearle's Antony.

This meant that the name of the play could be shortened to A & C and other familiar names could likewise be shortened to initials. I realised this was only a reprieve, but sufficient unto the day; the first hurdle was being negotiated; I was doing all right.

Of course what Edith needed was not a secretary but a dictaphone; in the years to come she never slackened speed until I cried for mercy. I knew I was a poor performer, but a Parliamentary stenographer would have had difficulty in coping. I used to feel that Edith was being plain selfish, unlike dear patient Dodie who would keep an eye on me and pause when she saw I was struggling along several sentences in arrears.

But on this day, and for many days to come, there was no question of criticism. Edith was perfect; I was the most fortunate secretary in London, albeit at the moment only temporary.

I took the letters home to type, then delivered them to the Piccadilly Theatre where Edith was rehearsing. A couple of days later she rang to ask if I would come to Albany after dinner to hear her words. I would, but my heart sank.

The intermittent stammer seldom worried me now, thanks to the late Elsie Fogerty, Principal of the Central School of Speech and Drama, then at the Albert Hall, to whom I had gone for help before the war. Many famous actors and actresses had gone to her when they were having voice trouble, including Sir John Gielgud, Dame Sybil Thorndike, and Edith herself. One day when I went for my lesson Fogerty told me that I was standing on the same piece of carpet on which Edith Evans had just stood.

At the Fire Station I never stammered, I was too afraid of being thought a cowardly telephonist stammering with fright. But I still thought of myself as a stammerer, and the fear that it might attack me at an inopportune moment was always with me.

As all stammerers know, there are certain words that refuse to be spoken. One can usually substitute an easier word, though as Fogerty explained: 'It's not that you can't say a word, but that you can't stop saying it.' For instance lo-o-o-ve.

Aldous Huxley wrote a brilliant short story called 'Half-Holiday' in which the wretched young man was a stammerer. He was forced to substitute pussy for cat, hound for dog, and a mug of mocha for a cup of coffee. I could hardly follow his example when hearing Edith's words; my new career would be over before it was begun.

But it looked as if my Waterloo might be postponed. As I dressed to go down to Albany a violent thunderstorm broke. The rain fell in torrents, lightning flashed, thunder rolled. I waited for the telephone to ring and for Edith to cancel our engagement.

How little I knew Edith! Fog, snow, ice, she ignored them all. In the same way she ignored pain and sickness. The show always went on, at least until the advent of *Nina* nine years later.

I waited as long as I dared, then went down into the street, prepared to walk, as American servicemen with their enormous tips were still the taximan's favourite fare. But an empty taxi did come along and all too soon I was in Albany, and there was Edith standing by the windows, wearing a green velvet housecoat and holding a red Temple Shakespeare in her hand. She was ready to begin.

I was not ready. 'I'm sorry,' I said, 'I should have told you; I have a stammer which makes it impossible for me to hear your words.'

'I'm not interested in your stammer,' answered Edith, 'I'm only interested in having my words heard.' And handing me the book she sat down.

Although I did not know it, it was a typical Edith remark. Nothing and no one could deflect her from her purpose, and that night her purpose was to have her words heard.

There was no question of argument, it never occurred to me, and anyhow I felt confident. It was a miracle, miraculously permanent, and through eleven plays covering twenty-five years, and without the murmur of a stammer, I heard Edith's words with mutual benefit to us both.

Chapter Three

Antony and Cleopatra was scheduled for a long prior-to-London tour. Theatres were hard to come by in 1946. Some, like the Shaftesbury and the Queen's, had been bombed, and there was a queue of plays waiting to come in.

It was from Leeds that Edith wrote to say that her secretary, a war widow, was to marry again, and if I wanted the job it was mine. On some sort of part-time basis, she explained, as there was not enough work for a full-time job, and also she wanted to keep her car in commission without increasing her overheads.

This sounded perfectly reasonable to me, but a friend to whom I showed the letter found it hilariously funny that Edith should rate her secretary such a poor second to her car.

Of course at this time I knew nothing of Edith's obsession with all matters financial, but it was a subject which greatly concerned her. She discussed it at length, deploring her overheads, commitments and responsibilities, later blaming me for having no responsibilities.

Edith's friends found this obsession very frustrating and exceedingly boring. Edith led such an interesting life, met so many remarkable people, it would have been instructive to learn more of Mrs Pandit Nehru and Mrs Eleanor Roosevelt; and Dame Rebecca West, though here Edith did make the illuminating statement that she felt that she was attending a lecture and should have taken a notebook and pencil to record Dame Rebecca's flow of conversation for posterity. But no – Edith preferred to discuss her wages bill.

It was easy to scoff, but not so easy to think oneself into the mind of a woman, born into a poor family, who had by her own unaided efforts risen to the head of her profession and in the process earned every penny she possessed. No wonder Edith had a highly developed sense of the value of money, and a subconscious antagonism towards people who had money without having worked for it. Had she a fear of poverty? I think so. If she had been a happy-go-lucky type who could take overdrafts and debts in her stride, this facet of her character would never have come to the fore, but despite her incomparable playing of Restoration comedy Edith was predominantly serious-minded.

She was not a mean woman, far from it. She compared herself to Ellen Terry who grumbled over spending sixpence, then gaily gave away hundreds of pounds. Edith too gave away a great deal, privately and unbeknown, and lent quite large sums, knowing the money would never be returned. There was one particular instance when an actress-friend's bank account was in difficulty and Edith sent me off on a pouring wet afternoon to pay a cheque into the bank. When the friend was again in work I waited for the loan to be repaid. It never was, but the friendship remained as warm as ever.

When the tour of *Antony and Cleopatra* ended and Edith returned to Albany, there was still a short while to go before the London first night. During this time I met Edith's ex-secretary.

Peggy was a witty and attractive young woman who had come to Edith on the introduction of a mutual friend, mainly because she wanted to be in London, and as she had many friends her social life must have conflicted with her duties, which I gathered were multifarious. She gave me a warning. 'Never,' she said, 'take on any extra chores unless you are prepared to carry on indefinitely.'

I thanked her for the advice which I had no intention of taking. It was impossible to imagine a time or a situation where I would not be willing to give my all for Edith. In fact I started straight away, not so much giving as giving up. There were certain habits of mine which were not compatible with life as lived in L 4, Albany.

I had first met Dodie at the Three Arts Club where to have called her Miss Smith would have been absurd. But Edith was always to remain Dame Edith, and when I called her darling, which was not unusual in the theatre, she told me not to, as 'it was bad for discipline'. In the same way it would be bad for discipline if I called her Edith.

Then there was the matter of a mid-morning cup of coffee which Dodie's housekeeper had always brought me, but when I heated up and drank the remains of Edith's breakfast coffee, it was coffee that she had been looking forward to drinking later. And lastly there was smoking while I worked: as Edith hated the smell of cigarettes that habit had to go. I suffered this loss of freedom with equanimity. To be with Edith was enough.

There was one way in which working for Edith was a revelation. She never failed to introduce me to everyone, whether they came to Albany or whether they were met outside. Dodie had never done this and I found it highly embarrassing as I stood first on one leg and then on the other, wondering whether or not to join in the conversation. It had the effect of making me feel diminished, whereas with Edith I felt enlarged.

Antony and Cleopatra opened at the Piccadilly Theatre on 20 December, and I was interested to see how Edith would react to a first night. Dodie had always remained remarkably calm, but by the first night a playwright's work is done, nothing he can do can change anything.

I expected an actress to be more dramatic, perhaps a display of fireworks, but to my surprise Edith spent most of the day in the sitting-room unravelling the knots in a box of string – string being then in short supply. But if Edith had not been sorting string she would certainly not have been giving a firework display. I was to learn that the more nervous and apprehensive she was the quieter and more withdrawn she became.

For this first night Edith had given her housekeeper and myself seats in the Stalls, but I would have been happier with my friends up aloft. The atmosphere down below was unsympathetic and I knew the reason why. I had friends in the theatre and they all said that Edith was too old to play Cleopatra and should never have attempted it. It was my introduction to that wretched question of age which was to recur so often during our time together.

The notices were a mixture although most critics praised the production, and the highly colourful settings and costumes by the Motleys, three talented women who had been in the first flight of stage-designers since the early thirties. Glen Byam Shaw was the director, a very dear friend whom Edith trusted completely, and it was during this production that he said to her: 'Whatever happens, and whatever anyone says, never forget that you are a great actress.'

Anthony Cookman, then drama critic of *The Times*, echoed these sentiments when he wrote: 'Dame Edith Evans is not, perhaps, the whole of Shakespeare's Cleopatra, but how accomplished is the portrait she paints of Egypt's queen. Every stroke of the brush, whether mockery, cajolery, or royal dignity be the motive, it is a joy to watch, and she speaks the lament over Antony with exquisitely moving grace.' 920 EVA/ B47952

James Agate was more carping, saying that Godfrey Tearle and Edith Evans were both miscast. But I remember this Cleopatra with affection. Edith may have been too old (she was fifty-eight) but she spoke the words so beautifully that age was unimportant, as we are told was the case with Duse and Ellen Terry.

The run of the play was not helped by the intense cold, a winter that no one who suffered it will ever forget. The discomfort was aggravated by the impossibility of buying warm clothing; not only were coupons needed but the goods were not in the shops. My snow-boots had not outlived the war, and I was obliged to buy boots soled with hinged wooden slats which acted like toboggans on the ice as I slithered my way down George Street to Piccadilly. Electricity was rationed, not by being turned off at the mains – no one had yet thought of that one – but by the co-operation of the public who were asked not to use heat or light at certain specified times. Edith was, of course, co-operative, and we duly froze. In the same way heating was prohibited in public places, including theatres, and audiences would arrive muffled in sweaters and carrying rugs, whilst on the stage Edith begged the actors not to fling their cloaks over their shoulders as the draught they made was like a blast from Antarctica.

So, all things working against it, the play had a difficult time, and as there were always empty seats I could sit at the back of the dress circle whenever I had the time. *Antony and Cleopatra* became my favourite and most familiar of Shakespeare's plays.

Felix Topolski painted a huge picture of the production (reproduced in the ninth *Saturday Book*), a great swirl of flamboyant colour with Edith as the central figure. She bought the picture for two hundred pounds, a lot of money in those days, but it was worth it. I had never admired Topolski's work but I would have liked this picture for myself.

I went with Edith to his studio, approached through a wicket-gate and an overgrown garden. It was romantic, though probably extremely damp, with windows on a level with the Regent's Canal. Sitting in the window-seat one could watch the barges passing by.

It was during this time that I was introduced to Chloe, the car to which I had been rated a poor second, though I was steadily climbing in the charts. Godfrey Tearle had garaged Chloe at the Cumberland Hotel where he was staying, after he and Anthony Quayle, who played Enobarbus, had travelled with Edith on tour, sharing the driving between them.

On this day Edith was not looking her best. Later I was to become familiar with the way her off-stage personality was coloured by the fact of her being either happy or unhappy in the part she was playing. Now she was unhappy, an undistinguished middle-aged woman sitting beside a pillar in the foyer, unrecognised by the crowd jostling around her.

With the arrival of Godfrey Tearle she recovered some of her natural ebullience, as any woman would have done. He was a splendid-looking man with the most beautiful speaking voice I ever heard. A perfect example, as I imagined it, of the old-time actor. We went out with him to collect Chloe.

Chloe was a cream-coloured 25-hp Chrysler with a drop-head coupé, a glamorous car for those dreary days and one which I was to enjoy driving until Edith decided that I was becoming too proprietary. Calling a car by name was one of Edith's few sentimentalities, but this car was particularly dear as a reminder of her husband Guy who had died in 1935, and of Washenden their country home at Biddenden in Kent. Whether this was the original Chloe I cannot say, but I have an idea that they were numbered I, II and III.

It is no use pretending that Edith was a good driver; she was not. She had learnt too late in life, when the war started and her chauffeur was called up. Certainly she had passed her driving test after several attempts, and after having been taken in hand by a young man who must have been a little in love as he told her she was a good driver, a remark which she quoted whenever I, as passenger, started to panic. The trouble was that she had no traffic sense and was completely fearless, during the blitz driving every weekend from London to Washenden, with only a pin-point of headlights and with bombs falling. It must have been a terrifying experience, one I would never have attempted, but all alone Edith did it.

I admired her courage but it did not make driving with her any easier. Fortunately this was 1947 with petrol rationing and few cars on the road, but even the drivers of these few cars hooted angrily as Edith waved them on or waved them down with wildly erratic and highly individual hand signals.

I have heard it said that Dame Gladys Cooper was a hair-raising driver, whilst Margaret Leighton, who at this time lived in Albany, had a name for being pretty terrifying in her powerful Jaguar. Perhaps star actresses are not mentally equipped to make star drivers.

Chapter Four

No tears were shed when *Antony and Cleopatra* closed on 8 March 1947, after a run of just over two months. It was a particular joy to Edith, leaving her free to take her first real holiday for over six years. This was not peculiar to Edith; a country at war was not an ideal holiday resort.

This 1947 holiday was already planned: a visit to South Africa to stay with her friend Gwen Ffrangcon-Davies in Pretoria, with treks to the Game Reserve, the Victoria Falls, Johannesburg, Cape Town, and other points including Rhodesia. But before this Edith was to spend a week in Brussels with her long-time friend Muriel Adams, who as Muriel Dole had played with her in *Troilus and Cressida* in 1912. Muriel had since married into the Diplomatic Service and her husband 'Budge' was now *en poste* in Brussels.

I remember this visit for several reasons, the first being Croydon Airport. Croydon was then the main, perhaps the only London airport, and I drove Edith there in Chloe. The airport buildings were prefabricated huts and the security was strict, so much so that I was not supposed to accompany Edith to the departure lounge, which was just another hut furnished with wooden benches. But Edith was looking tired and I persuaded the officials to let me sit with her in the hut which appeared to be filled with refugees; all with head-scarves; all wearing shabby and ill-fitting garments; all on their way home after years spent in a foreign country. In 1947 the war and its aftermath was still very much with us.

My second reason for remembering this Brussels visit was a poem

24

I sent to Edith, or rather a piece of doggerel verse, something about how much she was missed in Albany. Fortunately I can only remember one line: 'The rope walk's very lonely now our Dame has gone away.' I blush at the thought, but the fact was that in the Fire Service my verse had been much appreciated; I wrote it for all occasions. But Edith was a true professional: her friends were all professionals in their particular fields. She disliked amateurs. As she said of amateur theatricals: 'There's no harm in them as long as they don't expect me to watch them.' There was an occasion, years later, when the young son of a friend stayed with her in the country. He talked at length on music, piano-playing in particular, from which we gathered that he was a more than passable executant. So Edith hired a piano, only to find that he was nothing more than a passable strummer. She never again mentioned the matter, neither did she mention my doggerel, but from hints dropped I gathered that it had not been appreciated. It was a mistake I did not repeat. I might mention that Dodie enjoyed my verse; perhaps it was not all that bad.

When Edith returned from Brussels it was time for her South African journey. This visit, which was to be several months' duration meant that she would be away on her Father's birthday, so it was arranged that I should go with her to Eastbourne to be introduced to Mr Evans, then deputise for her on the birthday, taking a collection of goodies, including a bottle of champagne for the birthday luncheon.

Peggy had described Mr Evans as a dear old man, very cockney, very Dickensian, intensely proud of his famous daughter. Peggy also said that the 'famous daughter' might have visited her father more often, but when I first knew Edith she went down to Eastbourne every Sunday. She certainly never stayed the night; why should she? But for a working actress to give up her only free day was indeed a sacrifice. It was Edith's example which made me more aware of my own family, whom I had treated abominably, often not seeing them for months, even years, at a time. Edith had a great sense of family, and her father was particularly dear as being her only close relative, her brother having died as a child and her mother in the same year as Guy. She craved relations, however remote, and went to great lengths to gather them in from distant parts.

Having been with Edith so short a time I had not yet worked this out when we started off on our journey to visit Mr Evans in Victoria Drive, Eastbourne.

It was a glorious day for a drive, but before getting under way we stopped for petrol at a filling station in Buckingham Palace Road. The car in front of us had just filled up when a woman jumped out and ran across to where Edith and I were waiting in Chloe. 'I absolutely adore you!' she cried, smiling all over her nice face, then ran back to her car and drove away with her husband.

This was the kind of 'fan' of whom Edith approved. In 1938 I had written her a 'fan letter', the only one I ever wrote, and she replied to the effect that mine was the sort of letter she liked, but that some fan letters made her feel a bit sick. I shall have more to say of the other sort later.

In this outward journey to Eastbourne I was driving (we kept a strict rota of turn and turn about) while Edith slept as she always did in a car, but never so deeply as not to wake if I drove too fast. During her wakeful periods she spoke of her mother and father, of her work as a milliner, and of Guy and Washenden.

I was to learn a great deal about Edith during these drives together. Miss Elizabeth Salter, who during the last years of Dame Edith Sitwell's life was her secretary, and in 1967 wrote a book entitled *The Last Years of a Rebel*, was surprised that Dame Edith Sitwell should have discussed with her so many intimate details of her life. I was not surprised, having listened to my Dame Edith over the years.

But the reaction these talks aroused in me was not always that which Edith intended, particularly when she spoke of her parents. Instead of making them sound attractive they sounded to me unattractive, and the traits which Edith found admirable I found the reverse. They had obviously tried to contain her natural boisterousness, and what she told me in 1947 was much the same as she told Derek Prouse in 1961 in an interview published in a three-week series in the *Sunday Times*. She had a high regard and affection for Derek Prouse and the interview was streets ahead of any written since, or recorded on radio or television. Speaking of her mother she said: 'She used to watch me as I came down the street. "Swinging those arms," she'd say. Well-bred girls didn't swing their arms, neither did they laugh loudly, both of which I did. "Not so loud, my child!" I can still hear her voice now.'

It sounded very inhibiting, but Edith could have borne no ill-will

26

or her affection for her parents could not have proved so lasting, and of course it was the Victorian era when children were seen but not heard and parents would not be expected to have a perceptive understanding of a daughter. And what overwhelming perception would have been needed by an ordinary working-class couple on finding they had given birth to a human dynamo. They cannot be blamed for not realising that they had also given birth to a genius. But in a later passage of the interview there is a poignant statement made by Mrs Evans and quoted by Edith: 'Years after, when she was an old lady, she once said to me with tears in her eyes: "We didn't know, child, we didn't know." '

A question I longed to ask when Edith was talking of her childhood, was whether as a child she had had a cockney accent. Unfortunately I never brought myself to ask; it would have been lèse-majesté. But with a cockney father, and attending a church school – St Michael's, Chester Square – fees sixpence a week, it seems likely. Early in my days with Edith I met a chum from this same school who called her Ede, but there again I missed my opportunity to question her.

So the puzzle of Edith's accent remains unsolved, but if she had one it must have been cured when, at the age of sixteen, she joined Miss Nell Massey's dramatic classes which led to her playing Cressida in William Poel's production of *Troilus and Cressida*. It was on the drive to Eastbourne that Edith told me of dashing home from the millinery where she worked, putting on an apron, taking up the lodger's dinner, then running all the way over Ebury Bridge to her classes.

Her recollections of the millinery also included jumping about and falling through a glass roof, and of delivering a hat to a lady in Belgrave Square. On this occasion she was directed to the back door and the back stairs, but when the lady met her she apologised saying: 'Oh, I'm so sorry, I didn't know that you were one of us.' So even then Edith must have worn her clothes with an air, and surely did not have a cockney accent if she was 'one of us'.

I could picture Edith as a girl, as a milliner, and at drama classes, more readily than I could picture her as a married woman with Guy at Washenden. Marriage was alien to her single-minded absorption in her profession.

Guy always remained an enigma. Edith told me that Bernard

Shaw once said: 'I don't believe in this husband of yours; I don't believe you have a husband', which sounded as if Guy took no part in her professional life. But mutual friends told me he was not a weak man, rather he had a strong will of his own, and was very much a countryman glorying in cutting down trees and working in the garden. In his case Edith must have lifted her ban on smoking, in every photograph he is seen smoking a pipe. But again, as with her parents, Edith applauded traits in his character which I found unattractive, such as his dislike of being asked where he had been, or what he had done, or what he intended doing.

But Edith obviously adored him. I am sure he must have been a physically attractive man and Edith must have suffered the natural jealousies of any woman forced to leave her man for six days of the week. She told me of the housemaid who came out of the bathroom, naked under her dressing-gown, flaunting her figure. 'I wanted to kill her,' she said.

It was not only of Guy and her parents Edith talked. I also learnt some of her dislikes, such as her distaste for dirty stories. I never heard anyone tell Edith even a pale blue joke, but she told me that when she was entertaining the troops abroad, with a company that shall be nameless, she suffered acute embarrassment and the unhappy feeling of being the odd man out, as she was forced to listen to a non-stop stream of dirty stories and innuendoes, not from the troops, but from her fellow artists. Edith believed that people who revelled in dirty stories had had an unsatisfactory sex life. Hers had been satisfactory.

It was no deprivation to me not to tell dirty stories – I hated them – but it was a deprivation not to be able to discuss my first nights and criticise the performances. Edith never voiced her dislike of this, there was no need, her face registered her strong disapproval that I, an amateur, should criticise members of her profession. I respected her point of view and thereafter kept mine to myself. But after a while when we got to know each other better, she came to realise that although I was not a professional in her sense of the word, I was a professional theatre-goer and knew what I was talking about. After this it was possible to discuss the plays amicably, and she would even repeat my opinions to her friends with 'Jean says . . .'

Some while ago I overheard a really frightening remark from a woman who had been to the theatre and was discussing it with a friend. 'I go to the theatre to enjoy myself,' she said. 'I'm not one of those people who go to criticise.' But surely to be critical is the very essence of enjoyment, not only in the theatre but in every form of art.

I have strayed from our drive to Eastbourne where we reached the little house in Victoria Drive about lunchtime. The door was opened by Potter, Edith's old maid, who was on a visit. 'He's gone, miss,' she said. 'He's gone.'

I realised that Mr Evans had died, but Edith did not. 'Gone where?' she asked. Then Potter told her that Mr Evans had gone out earlier to do some shopping and had fallen down dead in the street.

A merciful way to die, but a terrible shock to Edith. The remainder of the day is a blur, but I have a vivid recollection of sitting in Chloe outside the mortuary while Edith went in to identify the body. Coming out she was terribly upset, as was only natural, but what had upset her most was the fact that no one had tidied up the old man and that his face was covered in dirt and blood from his fall. Edith kept on repeating: 'He always kept himself so clean; he was such a clean old man.' But she was spared the distress of making the funeral arrangements; this was done by Dr McAleenan, Mr Evans's doctor, a considerate and understanding man.

We must have had lunch, the lunch we should have shared with Mr Evans, but I cannot remember it, neither can I remember the drive home except that again I was driving. Back in Albany Edith dictated a cable to Gwen saying that the visit must be postponed.

In the morning Gwen rang from Pretoria. It was a typically warm-hearted gesture, but as Gwen was renowned for talking at an unprecedented speed it was impossible to understand more than the occasional word, and equally impossible to get a word in edgeways. Despite the tragedy of yesterday, Edith and I had to laugh.

I drove Edith to the funeral in Chloe, afraid that I might drive into the back of the hearse or stall the engine. The little cemetery chapel was crowded with Mr Evans's friends and neighbours, proving that he must have been a much-loved old gentleman. The only discordant note was struck by the clergyman who conducted the service, and who shared a joke with the undertaker's men as they walked towards the grave. I felt, perhaps unjustly, that he would not have behaved in this way had Mr Evans been a man of wealth and standing.

That night I wrote to a friend that Edith stood like a soldier at the graveside. The friend, not sharing my admiration for Edith, replied that she disapproved of daughters who stood like soldiers at their father's graveside. This was very much as I had felt when Edith praised Guy and her parents, proving that what we find laudable others may find despicable.

Mr Evans's death was a tragic loss to Edith, and for days after the funeral I would come into her bedroom in the morning to find her in tears. Very silent tears which trickled down her cheeks in little streams.

What she needed was the complete change of South Africa, but first there were several visits to Victoria Drive to help Miss Norton, Mr Evans's housekeeper, clear up the house. On one of these visits we took Winifred Oughton, an extremely competent character actress and a teacher at RADA, who was Edith's oldest friend. Winifred's character was as forceful as Edith's which sometimes led to sparks flying; they flew one night in 1956 when Edith was playing in *The Chalk Garden* at the Haymarket Theatre and had invited Winifred to drive down with her to the country and stay the weekend. Winifred arrived at the theatre with her suitcase, but as Edith was still on the stage she waited in her dressing-room. This sounds a sensible thing to do and Winifred was used to waiting in the dressing-room of her beloved friend Yvonne Arnaud so that they could travel together to Effingham where they both lived. But Edith had not Miss Arnaud's happy disposition and strictly adhered to the rule of no visitors back stage during the performance. So finding Winifred sitting on her settee she blew up and ordered her to wait outside. Winifred, justifiably hurt and angry, not only went outside but took a bus to Waterloo, and a train home to Effingham. It was a long time before the rift was healed.

But on this day there was no rift; the only one to take umbrage was Miss Norton who was reduced to tears as Winifred threw out pot after pot of home-made jam, declaring it was mouldy. Edith, on the other hand, saw no harm in mould, and over the years I ate my share of mouldy jam, Edith insisted that it was beneficial as it contained penicillin.

On one occasion Edith and I stayed the night in Victoria Drive, and in the evening went for a long walk over the downs to East Dean. I considered myself a good walker having been trained in the hard school of Welsh mountains, but Edith, though walking slower, could travel vast distances without tiring, leaving me panting at the finish.

At last everything was settled and Edith was free to fly to South Africa. I went with her to the Air Terminal and while we waited for the coach a young man came and sat down beside us. 'Ought I to know you?' he asked Edith. 'I don't think so,' she answered sweetly. 'Oh, I just wondered,' said the young man, 'one sometimes meets interesting people here.'

He went on to tell us that he was a reporter. If so he was the chubbiest, cubbiest cub-reporter that ever was. After a while he left us to look for someone really interesting.

When it was time for the coach to leave there was no room for me to travel with Edith to Heathrow. I stood in the passenger lounge watching as she went through the door – so white, so tired, so forlorn. No wonder the young reporter had not recognised her.

Chapter Five

With Edith in South Africa I was free to explore Albany, or at least that part of it which was L 4. Edith had moved there in 1940 when the black-out made it increasingly difficult to cross the wastes of Belgrave Square on her way from the theatre to her home in West Halkin Street. She had already told me of the move, and of how when the furniture arrived she was forced to give half of it away to the removal men when it became apparent that L 4 could not hold another stick. Miss Marguerite Steen had adopted the same tactics when moving from London to the country, and wrote in a volume of autobiography: 'I picked out suitable pieces and flung the residue to the removal men.'

Whether Edith's discarded furniture held any treasure I cannot tell; the furniture in Albany certainly did. From drawers in the tall-boy, pigeon-holes in the desk, dress boxes and hat boxes, I unearthed press cuttings, letters, photographs and snapshots. Perhaps they had been stored away for the move, but if so it was strange that Edith should let seven years elapse without sorting them out. It was more likely that they had been in their present hiding-places for many years, and would have remained there still if an inquisitive creature like myself had not come on the scene. I already knew that Edith was not interested in the past except in so far as it concerned Guy or her parents. It was the present and future which concerned her; old parts and triumphs were dead wood, and like dead wood kindled no flame.

I started with the letters. They were rewarding, many from

Popperfoto

At home in Albany, 1945

Walking in Leeds, 1950 (*l. to r.*), the author, John Van Dreelan, Dame
Edith

Bernard Shaw, and from the novelist George Moore who had been so impressed by Edith's performance in William Poel's production of *Troilus and Cressida* in 1912 that he later asked her to appear in his play *Elizabeth Cooper*. There were also letters from great players of the past, including Ellen Terry and Mrs Patrick Campbell. There was even the fan letter which I had written in 1938; not many secretaries find themselves in such a Hall of Fame.

There were other letters, equally rewarding and more moving. These correspondents were not so famous, though some became so; at this time they were young men who had left the theatre to fight in Hitler's war and writing to Edith was their life-line to sanity. To her they poured out their present frustrations and hopes for the future. It may sound shocking that I should have read these letters, perhaps it was, but my overwhelming interest in everything concerning Edith stifled my finer feelings.

I was to meet some of these young men later when they came to Albany. At first they came often, then less and less, then not at all. It was the wives. The disparity in age was too great for them to feel jealous, but Edith generated so much vitality that they must have felt at a disadvantage. No young woman could willingly allow this to happen. They struck camp and departed, taking their husbands with them.

But there was one male follower whom Edith could have done without. He was a critic, much addicted to alcohol and now long dead, who would arrive uninvited in the evening. I was living in Albany at the time and Edith would ring me to come down immediately and 'play gooseberry'. She had already explained that if she was left alone with this character he would have her on her back in a trice. So there I sat, occasionally going into the kitchen to make coffee, being careful to leave the door open, and while I was out of the way he would mutter: 'Why doesn't she go? Send her away.' But I stayed until, angry and frustrated, he was forced to leave.

From the letters I moved to the photographs and snapshots. These were a biographer's dream, dating back to when Edith was a girl on holiday at the seaside, and in those faded sepia prints her vitality jumped out at one as she sat on the shingle laughing into the camera. There was also a photograph of *Tiger Cats* with Edith reclining voluptuously on a tiger skin; and of course there were snapshots of her father and mother, and of Guy with his eternal pipe.

It was these snapshots which formed the nucleus of the scrap-books which I then started to make, and which were used nearly thirty years later in the television film Edith made with Bryan Forbes.

Whoever wrote the article on the production in the *TV Times* took it for granted that Edith herself had made the scrapbooks, and wrote: 'The past exists in a few portraits of her on the wall, and in two very thick green-bound scrapbooks of letters, photographs and cuttings, pasted neatly but at random, so that there is no progression of dates.' But how could there be progression when it was to be years before I finally found the last of these treasures.

The press cuttings, which were mostly in the dress boxes, were in a terrible state, many of them brown and brittle with age. Some actors insist that they never read their notices, although one is pretty sure that they take a peek when there is anything worth read-ing. But Edith genuinely never read them and only spasmodically belonged to a press cutting agency. But now I took these old cuttings, none of them in date order, sorted them and tied them into brown-paper parcels, which like the scrapbooks had their uses in 1954 when J. C. Trewin wrote his illustrated study of Dame Edith's work.

I enjoyed myself enormously; what I did not enjoy was super-vising the work being carried out in L 4. Interior decorating had been impossible during the war and was not much easier in 1947, with shortages all round making a splendid excuse for slowing down if not grinding to a halt. In the case of the upholsterer the excuse was Queen Mary. Our upholsterer was also Queen Mary's, and our work was held up for several days at a time when he sneaked off to Marlborough House which was being re-carpeted and curtained after Queen Mary's war-time evacuation to the country. The trouble was that we had three months in which to complete the job, and everyone except me treated this as if it was three years. I suffered extreme frustration.

During this time Potter was still at Eastbourne with Miss Norton, but later she came up to help with the cleaning, and it was from her that I learned something of Edith's in-laws. Before this the only in-law whom Edith had mentioned was a sister-in-law who sometimes acted as housekeeper at Washenden when Edith was playing in London, and once made the remark that a certain soap powder must be good 'as the advertisements speak so well of it'.

But what Potter told me as she polished the tallboy and as I sorted papers on the floor, was that Guy's family had deeply resented Edith. It could not have been snobbery as Edith and Guy had known each other from childhood which presupposes that they came from the same social background. Guy also attended Miss Massey's drama classes, presumably to be with Edith as he was destined for a mining engineer and not an actor. Why then did his family object? Was it because when Guy married he was lost to them? Or was Edith too possessive? She had a streak of possessiveness where her affections were concerned. Whatever it was, the family won in the end.

In 1934 Edith was to play the Nurse to Katherine Cornell's Juliet at the Martin Beck Theatre in New York. Guy had been ill for some time and there was a question as to whether Edith should stay with him and cancel the engagement, but he improved and she left for New York. As soon as she was out of the way Guy's family descended on Washenden, and despite Potter's protestations (she had been left in charge) carried him off to their home in Sheffield where he died later of a brain tumour. Edith had already been warned of his deteriorating condition and received the news of his death as she was boarding the ship to return to England – in those days there was no regular Atlantic air service. When she landed the funeral had already taken place. Edith found it difficult to forgive the family for not waiting for her, and for not letting her see her beloved husband for the last time.

That was Potter's story which I have no reason to doubt, and as for many years she played an important part in Edith's life, the rest of this chapter shall be hers.

Potter had been Mrs Evans's maid, and when Mrs Evans died Potter promised her never to leave Edith. She kept her promise but also kept her independence.

When I knew Potter she was an indomitable old lady, and I use the word 'lady' deliberately. When she died the wreath from her local Whist Club read: 'To a very great lady.'

At the time of which I am writing Potter would come down from Kilburn every afternoon to do Edith's washing and ironing, and any mending there might be. On Thursdays she came late as it was her day for buying the weekly meat ration in Sloane Street.

Sloane Street may sound a far cry from Albany, particularly as there was at least one excellent butcher in Brewer Street, but Potter had dealt there when Edith lived in West Halkin Street. It was an aristocratic establishment, now demolished to make way for the Carlton Towers, but no butcher could get the better of Potter, who even at her advanced age had a way with men.

She would return to Albany very pleased with herself. 'I told them that meat wouldn't do for my young lady,' she said. 'I told them only the best was good enough for my young lady', and she would show us some delectable cut off the joint, well beyond our ration.

When Potter died I suggested to Edith that she should go to the butcher, but as she could hardly expect to be recognised as Potter's 'young lady', I went. The visit was not a success. Edith's ration book was in her married name which meant nothing to the butcher, nor did he know Potter's name, only her personality. We fared badly.

It was not only with the butcher that Potter held her own. She jollied them along in Fortnum and Mason, not one wit abashed by morning coats and red carnations.

There was a story which Edith liked to tell of when Potter first went to West Halkin Street. It was a foreign country to her, although so close to Ebury Street where Edith had lived before. As Potter stood on the steps ready to go shopping, she looked right and left, then turned to Edith: 'Which way do I strike?' she asked.

Potter had other Potterisms. One was chimble. She would chimble the paper, which meant screwing the newspaper into spills before lighting the fire. Many years later I found the word 'chimble' in John Clare's *The Shepherd's Calendar*, where I read:

> *When mice from Terror's dangers nimbly run*
> *Leaving their tender young in fear's alarm*
> *Lapt up in nests of chimbled grasses warm*
> *Hoping for safety from their flight in vain.*

It was fascinating that an eighteenth-century word should be passed down to Mrs Potter of Kilburn.

I was surprised when Edith told me that Potter disliked me. She told Edith that I spied on her. I did not, but appearances were against me. I would often go shopping in the afternoon, and some-times when I reached the foot of the stairs I would remember a ration book or some other essential and have to run back for it. Edith would be out or away, and I would come in to find Potter enjoying a session in the lavatory with the door wide open. There was nothing wrong in that, but had she closed the door it would

36

have saved a lot of ill-feeling. As it was she thought I came back especially to catch her out.

It was not until Potter was ill in bed and I went up to her basement room in Palmerston Road, Kilburn, that I found that she had no lavatory, and had probably trained herself to wait until she reached Albany to perform in comfort.

There was little comfort at 29 Palmerston Road. The room was dark, deep below street level, the only furniture a dresser, an antique cooking-range, a couple of chairs and a table, and an immense iron bedstead with brass knobs at the four corners, where Potter must have lain with Mr Potter, conceiving and bearing thirteen children, all of whom died at birth.

I have no idea when Mr Potter died, certainly many years before my time, but as Potter liked to have a man around she found one for herself. He was probably a young man as when I later met his wife she was still a young woman. Potter evidently acquired him when she was working in West Halkin Street, for Edith told me that she would be wafted to the theatre on the delicious cooking smells of Potter preparing her young man's supper.

Why did Edith not protest? The reason was that she was sympathetic to any male–female relationship. She preferred men to women, her tragedy being that after Guy died she was dependent on women.

She understood married women, and many must remember with gratitude and affection her understanding when they were in trouble. I recall at least two women who came to Albany in deep distress after their husbands died, and went away comforted.

But unmarried women, particularly the not-so-young, were always potential lesbians. This was understandable. Edith suffered, as do most actresses, from embarrassing fan letters from a certain type of woman or young girl, and parts such as Sanchia Carson, the woman doctor in *Robert's Wife* or even Rosalind in *As You Like It*, where Edith made an enchanting young man in doublet and hose, appealed to this type. There was an evening in Albany when she had been sitting for a long while in the dark, on a stool in front of the fire, and having been her secretary for only a short while, and not knowing her ways, I thought she might be ill and came into the room saying: 'Are you all right? Is there anything I can do?' She rounded on me with: 'Damn you unmarried women!'

I put on my coat and went home. Almost immediately Edith rang to apologise. Knowing that her insinuations were wide of the mark I did not take umbrage, but it showed her distrust of any woman not involved in a love life. Had she had a male household, including a male secretary, she would have been far happier.

But to return to Potter and her young man. The friendship continued until the day of her death. I wish I knew where Potter first met him, but I do know that he visited her in Palmerston Road and drank the brandy the doctor prescribed and Edith paid for. I once said to Edith: 'How does Potter get through so much brandy? She can't possibly drink it all herself.' And Edith replied: 'It's Potter's brandy and she has the right to do with it as she pleases.'

While Potter was ill she made her will on a form bought from the local stationer. She understood her man, and knew that if she left him the money it would dissolve down his throat in drink, so she left it to his wife. Unfortunately she did not ask advice as to who should witness the will, and it was witnessed by the wife, the sole beneficiary, thus rendering it null and void. This is no place to go into details about the outcome; suffice to say that it resulted in much unpleasantness.

Potter died in a nursing home. On the evening that I took her there Edith rang to ask how she was. Potter answered the call on her bedside telephone, announcing with pride that she had had a lovely supper brought to her in bed. She was delighted to have had so much attention. That night she died in her sleep.

Potter's death was the end of an era; Edith's last link with the past of Mother, Father and Guy. Edith could talk to Potter as she could talk to no one else. There was not only affection between them, there was respect.

Potter was a wise woman who knew her young lady. When she came to Albany she never stayed a moment over her time, knowing that if she did it once it could become a habit, just as Peggy had warned me. Potter had her life apart from Albany, whist drives and coach trips, and of course her young man. But this did not detract from her affection for Edith. Many years before, when Edith was hard pressed for money, Potter took her savings out of the Post Office and offered them to her until times were easier.

Potter left a memorial, an imitation Waterford glass bowl of generous proportions, always known as Potter's bowl. It had been one of her many whist prizes and she always chose something which would be useful to Edith. And it was useful, in fact it was used continuously, and on the oak refectory table amongst the Georgian silver, could well be mistaken for genuine Waterford. As genuine as Potter herself.

Chapter Six

In the three months while Edith was in South Africa she wrote me seventeen letters and I wrote twenty-four; a mammoth correspondence, quite out of character with our output in the years ahead. But the circumstances were exceptional: Mr Evans's death had brought us closer together in a shorter space of time than would normally have been the case, and there was also the work being carried out in Albany which called for an exchange of question and answer.

The carbons, if any, of my letters have long since disappeared, but I know there were twenty-four as Edith would thank me for number so-and-so. Re-reading Edith's letters is a disappointment, but not a surprise. She once said, after dictating a letter: 'Anyone who keeps my letters will have a disappointment when I die. No one will want them; they're too dull.' And they were.

The fact was that Edith detested letter-writing; her mind worked so much faster than her pen, or my speedwriting, that she soon became bored and lapsed into the bare bones of reportage. This was the case during the two-thousand-mile tour which Gwen and Marda Vanne arranged for her, the itinerary of which I still possess, and which was headed 'A Month in the Country'. It included the Victoria Falls and the Kruger National Park.

Edith's first letters from Pretoria were very sad. The flight had been long and tiring, probably twice as long as it would be today, with overnight stops in gruelling temperatures. This added to her already deep depression which spilled over into her first letter written on what would have been her father's birthday. She recalls that it was already sixteen days since his death, showing that he must have been continually in her thoughts.

But as the days passed Edith was able to take an interest in her surroundings and to do some non-rationed shopping, a real excitement after six years of war. She wrote of buying a coat for £5 but not buying a dress for £35, as it was not well-cut and she preferred to wait and get 'a super one' from Molyneux. How much would Hartnell or Hardy Amies charge for that dress today? One of her more mundane purchases was yards of heavy mesh curtain net for the long Albany windows. Over the years I grew to loathe that net as I lugged the curtains up and down to wash them in the bath, until the day came when rationing was abolished and the heavy mesh gave way to nylon. But before this happened Sir Cecil Beaton came to Albany and took an enchanting picture of Edith against those same curtains, a picture reproduced in his book *Persona Grata*.

Our appalling winter was still fresh in Edith's mind and she told me to be sure to get all the coal that was our due and to order logs, if I could, from the Beales. The Beales were Kentish friends who lived at Sissinghurst Castle Farm, and Captain Beale was agent to Harold Nicolson and his wife Vita Sackville-West who lived at Sissinghurst Castle. Chloe and I made several journeys collecting logs but I was never very welcome, or so it seemed to me, and after a curt 'good-morning' was left to man-handle the logs as best I could. Later I discovered the reason, or thought I had, for my cold reception. During the war Edith had stored furniture with Mrs Beale which for years had taken up space which could have been used to better advantage.

On 29 May 'A Month in the Country' started and the letters became reportage, but there were some human touches. One of Edith's 'hates' was going to bed before midnight, but in South Africa, where people rose early, they also went to bed early, and on the tour, with car journeys averaging three hundred miles a day, sometimes as early as half-past eight. Edith's reaction was 'Horror!' and the result would be a white night. But even after a *nuit blanche* Edith was ready to join the party at half-past eight the following morning.

I say 'party' for there were friends of both Gwen and Marda on the tour, two of whom, Dr Harold Knox-Shaw and his wife Maisie, became dear friends of Edith's. Dr Knox-Shaw came from the Radcliffe Foundation at Oxford and was the head of the Radcliffe Observatory in South Africa. When the tour was over Edith stayed with them at The Cape where their small son Peter fell in love with her and wept bitterly at parting – his name for her was The Cosy Lady. Many years later they came to stay with Edith in Kent, by which time the 'small son' was an undergraduate at Cambridge where his uncle was Master of Sidney Sussex College. When Dr Knox-Shaw died Maisie visited England every summer and was a wonderful friend to Edith when she had her long heart illness in 1971.

Even before the end of the tour, in fact while they were still in the Game Reserve, Edith was starting to count the days to her return to England. She was tired of the continual packing and unpacking, and all through her life, wherever she was, her thoughts turned to home. In 1974 she was telling a reporter: 'It does matter to me to be in my own bed and my own bath.' So she wrote of there being only forty days left in Africa, then only thirty-seven, then thirty-three. Like a schoolgirl waiting for the end of term she made herself a calendar so that she could cross off the days.

This did not mean that Edith had not enjoyed herself; she was truly grateful for the holiday and wrote to that effect time and time again, but as her health improved and her vitality returned, her thoughts turned more and more, not only towards home, but to work in the theatre. She wrote that she was so full to the brim with life and strength that she should now be able to do great work. She felt capable of fine and wonderful things, and even asked me to say a prayer that she should be given the opportunity. But our combined prayers must have gone astray, for it was to be a year before Edith worked again, and almost two years before the triumph of *Daphne Laureola*.

On 25 July Edith wrote a final letter enumerating the fruit and groceries she would be bringing home, and of course that bundle of horrible curtain net. She asked me to try and come down to the Customs Shed at Southampton to meet her. She was returning by sea.

Chapter Seven

Edith did not enjoy the voyage home, the spirituous bonhomie of a large liner, with its rounds of drinks and sticky marks on the tables, was unattractive to a woman who seldom drank anything stronger than coffee. She had been warned beforehand that the boat was a very fashionable one, and had written that she hoped to keep out of the cocktail parties and just enjoy the sunshine. It must have been on her mind for in another letter she wrote that she could see herself dining in her cabin as 'I hate smart alecks'. Dodie and Alec had also disliked smart alecks, and in 1938 on the *Queen Mary*, then the Cunard's number one liner, had had bacon and eggs served in their cabin the better to avoid them.

I drove down to meet Edith at Southampton, a city not yet recovered from serious bomb damage. The only accommodation was in a private-hotel-cum-boarding-house, where Chloe spent the night in an overgrown vegetable garden, inhabited by a sinister character wearing baggy trousers and a Panama hat who kept popping up from behind the brussels sprouts. I fared little better in my bedroom which was festooned in cobwebs, some of which waved in the air above my head.

When Edith disembarked next morning I was leaning over the rail of the Customs Shed as arranged. How easy she was to pick out in the crowd, so tall and remarkable, no longer the forlorn figure to whom I had said goodbye, but gay and vivid and overflowing with energy.

The drive home was joyous as was Edith's appreciation of what had been done to L 4. It was a happy time with unpacking, presents all round, and oh such gorgeous food, the like of which we had not seen for seven years.

But it could not remain for ever a case of, 'let joy be unconfined'. Edith had written of being ready for fine work, and so she was, she looked wonderful, but as days and then weeks passed with no sign of work, she became increasingly low-spirited.

Edith's attitude to work was coloured by her upbringing in a working-class environment, where to be out of work was a disgrace. When I came into her bedroom in the morning with my notebook and pencil she would say: 'How glad I am that Father can't see me now; how distressed he would be that I'm not working.' And she would go on to say: 'Shall I never work again, Jean? Am I finished? Does no one want me anymore?'

I told her that of course she was not finished, that of course she would work again, and of course she was wanted. But I knew that was not strictly true. Her three appearances since the war in *The Rivals*, *Crime and Punishment*, and *Antony and Cleopatra*, had not really been successful.

In the case of *The Rivals*, I doubt if I was alone in finding it a bore. When I was at school in Eastbourne the town was visited annually by touring companies headed by Charles Doran and Henry Baynton. Until the age of fourteen one could only attend matinées, and as *The Rivals* was considered suitable for children and old ladies, I saw it countless times. Innumerable other children all over Britain must have done the same. We never recovered from it.

In *Crime and Punishment* Edith had played Katerina Ivanovna, a tiresome woman with a hacking cough who dies of consumption.

As for *Antony and Cleopatra*, Edith's appearance as Cleopatra had undoubtedly done her harm. There had been so much talk of age that she was now labelled a middle-aged actress.

This was illustrated by the affair of the Theatrical Garden Party, then held in Queen Mary's Garden, Regent's Park. All the stars attended and all were asked to do this or that. But this year no one asked Edith. When I rang the secretary of the Actors' Orphanage saying that Edith wished to help, the woman hedged a little and then suggested that Edith might join Dame Lilian Braithwaite. Edith was deeply hurt. She admired Dame Lilian, but Edith was a much younger woman. Dame Lilian called her the Junior Dame, which at that time she was. To bracket them together put Edith among the has-beens.

No wonder she was low-spirited, and I did my best to devise ways of helping her pass the time. I kept her supplied with books, and would bring my library book from the Times Book Club, or books from the Public Library, but she seldom did more than glance through them. The exception was anything by Dame Freya Stark with whom she seemed to have an affinity and whose books she much enjoyed.

There were, of course, books already in the shelves beside the fireplace. They were a heterogeneous collection. There were a great many signed copies, presented to Edith by the authors, which included Bernard Shaw and Richard Church, and Ellen Terry's *The Story of My Life* with the inscription: 'To Edith Evans, a girl after my own heart.' There was a complete edition of Proust which I am sure had never been opened, and Alexandre Dumas and Balzac in red leather editions which, when I was a girl, we gave to our friends as presents. These particular books gave me the idea that at some-time, someone, perhaps one of her young admirers, had tried to interest Edith in a course of reading, but judging by the immaculate glossiness of the covers he had not met with much success.

Museums and picture galleries were 'out'. Acting was the only art in which Edith was interested. Some years later when we were in Manchester for the prior-to-New York tour of *Daphne Laureola*, she came with me to the Manchester City Art Gallery where there was a splendid collection of Pre-Raphaelites, and those fascinating, or at least fascinating to me, huge Victorian Academy pictures. I could have stayed all day, but Edith blew through the gallery like a strong wind, barely pausing to look, and hardly had we entered before we left.

But on one occasion Edith did buy me a picture. We had been out together, and returning to Albany by way of Leicester Square we passed the Leicester Galleries, then in Irving Street. They were holding an exhibition of Artists of Fame and Promise, and the picture displayed on an easel in the window was by one of the promising artists. It was of a part of Hampstead Heath at night with a street lamp in the foreground, and the colours were sombre blues and greens. I stopped to admire, being at a stage of art appreciation when I admired sombre pictures. Some days later I visited the gallery to ask the price, only to be told that it was already sold. I told Edith of my disappointment and learnt that she had bought the picture for me.

It was a charmingly generous gesture, one which I should have done well to remember in the days ahead. But by then I had ceased to admire sombre pictures and instead bought John Nash and John Piper. My Artist of Promise, who I am sorry to say never fulfilled his promise, did not fit in, and I let him go. I should now like him back, but one can jog backwards only in memory.

If the days were difficult to fill, the evenings were worse. In the normal course of events Edith would have been starting for the theatre, but now a long, boring vista stretched ahead. This was when I lost many of my friends. I would put them off at the last moment when Edith asked me to go with her to a film or to dinner. It was a Royal Command, and anyhow I wanted to go; the idea of being a part-time secretary had long since been abandoned.

But the most difficult time was the weekends. In the past Edith had a country home as well as one in London, but now she was limited to chambers in Albany, which though delightful were small and cramped, not designed for living in for weeks on end. Edith was a large woman in every way, it chafed her intolerably to be cooped up in one place.

So the weekends became a nightmare. On Sunday there was nothing to do but roam London. Edith would take long walks in the City and often we would lunch together. There were few places to go, and one Sunday we went to the Charing Cross Hotel where she said how horrified her mother would have been to see her eating roast beef and Yorkshire pudding in a station hotel.

On another Sunday she walked up to my Baker Street flat so that we could again lunch together. After five years of living in Fire Stations the flat was my idea of heaven, but I now realise that it was low-ceilinged and dark, and to Edith, with her love of spaciousness, it was hell. She stood there like a trapped animal, with her head almost touching the ceiling, then without pausing to rest or sit down she turned and went back down the stairs. Perhaps 'fled' would be a better word.

There was nowhere for us to lunch except at a rather scruffy little café round the corner, and while we were there Edith said: 'I never thought I should be able to do this; I'm proud of myself for being able to do it.' It was a puzzling statement, but it must have summed up her feeling of horror at the meanness of her surroundings, and of having nothing better to do than take lunch with her secretary.

You may be asking, where were Edith's friends at this time? The fact was that she had few close friends. She found friendship difficult, there was an invisible barrier between herself and the easy give and take of friendship. Having been virtually an only child she had never had to share a bedroom, or toys, or put up with passed-down clothes.

But there were some close friends, and of these the closest were unfortunately out of England. There was Muriel Adams, who was still with her husband at the Brussels Embassy. There was Lucille Harris, who as Lucille Lisle had played with Edith in *The Late Christopher Bean*, but she was with her husband in New Zealand. There was also Winifred Oughton, but Winifred was busy with her teaching at RADA, as well as playing Mrs Durbeyfield in *Tess of the D'Urbervilles* at the Piccadilly Theatre.

Of course there were other theatre friends. There were dinner parties in Albany with Peggy Ashcroft and her husband Jeremy Hutchinson, George and Sophie Devine, Glen Byam Shaw and his wife Angela Baddeley. They all loved Edith dearly, but they had their own work, and their family ties of home and growing children.

It was a profoundly frustrating period for a woman who knew she had so much to give, yet was debarred from proving that she was still a great actress, indeed a greater actress than she had been in the past. There was a photograph of Edith taken in the garden at Washenden soon after Guy died, a picture of a sad, grey woman. That was how she looked now.

This may sound over-dramatic, but great actresses, whether in triumph or temporary oblivion, do react more dramatically than ordinary people. I have a bronze head, modelled by Hazel Armour, a friend of Athene Seyler, which shows a woman almost unbearably sad. Today, people say: 'Dame Edith could never have looked like that.' But she did.

We called it Jean's folly. When I went with Edith to the studio in Fitzroy Square, I rashly admired the head, and not until Hazel Armour had asked me over and over again if I meant to buy it, and written several times in the same vein, did I realise that I had landed myself with it. It cost seventy-five guineas, a sum which appalled me, but I am glad to report that over the years I became devoted to it, and unlike the Artist of Promise, was never tempted to dispose of it.

It was during this time that I went to live in Albany. Each set of chambers had a staff-room on the top floor, and there was a spare room in L block belonging to Mr Stone, an old gentleman known as the Squire of Piccadilly.

It was Edith's idea, though of course I was delighted. The fact was that she had removed her furniture from Sissinghurst Castle Farm and there were also some pieces from Victoria Drive. Some of them were very odd but, because they had belonged to Edith's dear ones, she thought them perfect. My only contribution was a large maplewood desk bought from Mr Ring of Brighton when Phyl and I were sharing a weekend flat in the long ago before the war.

Apart from the unrelated furniture my room was delightful, with a partition to make a tiny bedroom. There was a wash-basin, but as Albany prided itself on its antiquity, only cold water. But there was a bathroom along the passage with an immense copper geyser; it looked terrifying but was most efficient.

To live in Albany was a remarkable experience. Although in the heart of Piccadilly there was no sound of traffic, and lying in bed at night the only sound was of Big Ben striking and fog horns booming on the river.

Chapter Eight

Edith had come into contact with a number of theatrical people who were deeply concerned with the state of the world, and were left wing in their approach to politics. Edith had grown up in a left wing atmosphere. Her father had been pro-Boer in the South African war and was always an ardent socialist, whilst Guy had been President of the Biddenden Labour Party when they lived at Washenden.

Once at an election when Edith and I were walking along Brewer Street on the way to the polling station I said: 'We're wasting our time. You're going to vote Labour and I'm going to vote Conservative; we'll cancel each other out. Why don't we go home?' We did.

Most of the talk I heard at this time was idealistic and rather naïve. The Soviet Union was the hero of the piece and young men would come to tea to discuss Soviet art, Soviet culture, and the sacrifices made by the Soviets in the war. Not all of the young men were Communists, Edith certainly was not, but they believed that if the ordinary people of the Soviet Union and Britain could get together and learn to understand each other better, it would bring in the millennium.

At this time, unlike the pre-war period, it was fashionable to admire the Russians, all the best people did. Edith went to a dinner given by the Speaker of the House of Commons to meet a delegation of Russian women, and Vivien Leigh received the guests at a reception given by the Society for Cultural Relations with USSR, of which Edith was President. I remember this occasion vividly; as well as ending Edith an evening bag, I helped pin her into a pre-war Worth dress. It was the fault of those wretched clothing coupons, making it impossible for her to buy a new evening dress.

To help Edith keep in touch with all shades of opinion she read the *Daily Worker* as well as *The Times*. A year later, when she was having a great triumph in *Daphne Laureola*, Ivor Brown wrote a Profile of her for the *Observer* in which he said: 'Dame Edith is concerned with world-matters and reads the press of all parties, including the left wing. ("I want to see what they say.")'

I objected to the *Daily Worker* being delivered to Albany, just as many years later Edith was to object to the *Daily Express* being delivered to a friend staying with her in the country. At the time of the *Daily Express* débâcle I remembered the *Daily Worker* but was too tactful to mention it.

It was not only the politics of the *Daily Worker* which offended me, the paper was quite useless for lighting the fire. It may have been something to do with poor print or poor quality paper, but however industriously Potter chimbled, it refused to catch, and lay there smoking crossly. Today it would not have mattered, but at that time paper had to do the work of firewood.

It was while Edith was reading the *Daily Worker* and presiding over the Society for Cultural Relations, that she met the Soviet Minister of Culture who invited her to visit Moscow. She accepted with alacrity. But the arrangements were protracted, as Soviet arrangements still are, and I thought then, and think now, that she showed considerable courage in setting out alone behind the Iron Curtain.

Not having Edith's singleness of purpose I disliked my more mundane mission of going to the Soviet Consulate to collect her visa. It was the middle of the morning, but I was shown into a curtained room lit by artificial light, and was left alone with rows of empty red chairs and a portrait of Stalin scowling down at me. When at last I received the visa and was let out into the Bayswater Road, I gulped down great draughts of democratic air.

As Edith would be staying overnight in Prague, there was also a visit to the Czechoslovak Consulate. This was not frightening, but sad, with ill-clad, patient people, sitting on hard chairs awaiting their turn. Many looked as though they had waited an eternity, and I felt deeply apologetic and ashamed when I was shown in ahead of them.

There were no letters from Moscow as there had been from South Africa, only a postcard view of the Kremlin on which Edith had written that she might be one day late, and that I should tell Emlyn. (This reference to Emlyn Williams was connected with the shooting of his film *The Last Days of Dolwyn* in which Edith was to appear.)

The Moscow visit went off without incident, though I suspect it was the usual conducted tour, with – in Edith's case – the added bonus of some extremely decorative wooden boxes and several presentation jars of caviar. Edith disliked caviar but her friends made up for this strange aversion, and during this period dinner parties in Albany were extremely popular.

On her return I refrained from rushing at her and asking questions. I had been with her long enough to know that she, like Guy, disliked being asked what she had done or where she had been; like him she considered it an unwarranted intrusion of privacy.

But if I waited quietly and feigned lack of interest, I sometimes picked up crumbs of information. In this instance I picked up singularly little; she had seen Ulanova dance, she had walked round the Kremlin, she had visited Leningrad, and she had picked and brought home flowers from Tolstoy's garden – these I put in the scrapbook.

Perhaps it was Edith's dislike of museums and art galleries that made her recollections so unsatisfactory. Instead she spoke at length of her hats, which had intrigued her hosts. At this time she had several large hats with turned-back brims, there is a photograph of her wearing one of these on the cover of J. C. Trewin's book, and these must have taken the Muscovite women, whose only head-covering was a scarf, by storm. I imagine that all her clothes took them by storm, they were all Molyneux models.

One outcome of Edith's visit was a great disappointment to her. She had made friends, particularly with her young interpreter, and they had arranged to write. Edith wrote several times but never received an answer. In the end she gave up.

In July 1948, at the time of the Berlin Airlift, it ceased to be fashionable to admire the Russians. When Edith saw that her association with the Society for Cultural Relations might damage her theatrical career, she quietly dropped out. She never discussed the matter but it was plain to see.

Chapter Nine

Some time before the Soviet Minister for Culture invited Edith to visit Moscow, Emlyn Williams had been reading Jon Godden's *A House by the Sea*, and planned to make it into a film for Edith and himself.

It was the story of a love affair between two not-so-young people, but even with this proviso the film company who had bought the rights considered Edith too old. They asked her to make a test, a not unreasonable request as this would be her first film.

The test was shown in a little projection theatre in Golden Square, and I went there with Edith's agent Olive Harding, and two of Edith's South African friends.

It was awful. No one appeared to have done anything to make Edith look attractive, or studied her features, or gone to any trouble over her make-up. The result was that she looked far older than her age, and I can still see her on the screen, coming out of her little cottage, looking like someone's jolly but over-worked mother. As for the director, he must have been on holiday, otherwise he would surely have warned Edith that her stage approach was far too large for the screen. Perhaps that was what the company had hoped. The film was scrapped.

What Edith herself thought of the test I never knew. I asked no questions, and Edith never mentioned it then, or in the future.

But this was not to be the end of Edith's film career. Anatole de Grunwald invited her to tea at the Ritz and gave her the film script of *The Queen of Spades*.

Film scripts are quite unlike play scripts, being typed in columns, with the technical directions in one column and the dialogue in the other. This makes them difficult to read, so that when Edith read the script she said that the part offered to her, the Countess, was so small as hardly to be visible. It was certainly not a large part compared with Edith's stage parts: there was little dialogue, but there were long sequences when there was no need for words, her face would speak what was in her mind. The Countess's reactions were the pivot on which the film revolved. I pointed this out to Edith, marking her places in the script with red ink. She read it again and agreed to play the part.

Edith was grateful for what I had done, and told her friends that it was Jean who had persuaded her to play the part. For years I read her scripts and she respected my opinions, until the day came when I was proved terribly wrong and fell, like Lucifer, never to rise again.

The shooting of the film was an agony. This time Edith looked too young rather than too old, so the make-up department decided to use not greasepaint, but a liquid which dried into deep wrinkles. At the end of the day this was peeled off and, to Edith's horror, the wrinkles remained. She thought she was marked for life, which fortunately she was not, but as well as the wrinkles the liquid set up an intolerable irritation, so that when she came home from the studio her face was flaming red. Shooting had to be suspended until the irritation subsided, and until the make-up department thought up some lesser torture. But after this, and to spare her further agony, the shooting only took place once every three days.

Remembering that Edith created her own make-up for the part of the She-Ancient in Shaw's *Back to Methuselah* in 1924, and judging by the photographs made a magnificent job of it, the fuss over the Countess's wrinkles seems ridiculous. Given the tools Edith could surely have made a better job of it herself, particularly as when the film was shown the wrinkles looked absurdly unnatural.

Apart from the discomfort of the Countess's make-up, Edith enjoyed filming from the very first day. Being a poor sleeper, it was no hardship to be up at five o'clock in the morning. She got on well with the technicians and camera crew. They expected a Dame to be difficult, but instead she called herself a 'new girl', and looked to them to help her.

The only one with whom she crossed swords was not a technician or a camera man, but the star of the film, Anton Walbrook. When scenes were being shot in which the Countess was speaking to him but he was not in the picture, he saw no reason for coming down to the studio. But Edith did, she had no intention of speaking to a blank wall.

It was while Edith was finishing the shooting of *The Queen of Spades* that she received the invitation to visit Moscow, but before leaving she arranged that, on her return, she would play in a film written by Emlyn Williams. Emlyn knew how disappointed she had been over *A House by the Sea*, so he went home and wrote a film for her. It was called *The Last Days of Dolwyn*.

It was the story of a Welsh village that was to be drowned to make a reservoir for a city's water supply. It was of special interest to me as we had lived in the Conway Valley in North Wales when the Eigiau dam burst and destroyed the village of Dolgarrog. It happened at night, but from our house we could see the water pouring over the side of the mountain like a white sheet, and hear the rocks, that we saw later were the size of houses, crashing into the valley below.

Emlyn was to direct the film and came to Albany to read the script to Edith. I sat in on the reading and appreciated the way he wanted me, as well as Edith, to understand the story. As a boy, Emlyn came from a village near our colliery, the Point of Ayr. My Aunt Kate, who before most women took an interest in such things, was on the Council and the Board of Guardians, used to boast that she drove Emlyn Williams to school in her pony trap. I never repeated this to Emlyn, being sure that it was wishful thinking on the part of my aunt, but I did take a more than special interest in all that he did.

In this film Edith was to play the part of Merri, a part similar to that of Gwenny, the Welsh maid in *The Late Christopher Bean*, adapted by Emlyn from the French in 1933. Edith played both parts movingly. There was one particular scene in the film where Merri visits the rich landowner's wife to get her to save the village, and with her quiet countrywoman's dignity puts the woman to shame.

C. A. Lejeune, then the film critic of the *Observer*, wrote: 'She knows like a witch, how to drain her face and voice of everything she had learnt from fashion, and to start from innocence all over again.'

Unfortunately when *The Last Days of Dolwyn* was shown it was not a success, and ran only a couple of weeks at the Empire in Leicester Square, not the right cinema for it. The National Film Theatre might well give it a showing, as apart from Edith's performance it was Richard Burton's first film – he played Edith's son.

Chapter Ten

In 1948 Edith had made two films, had gone to Moscow, and now was to act again.

The Old Vic was still in its wartime home at the New Theatre, and Laurence Olivier and Vivien Leigh were taking the resident company on a tour of Australia and New Zealand. While they were away John Burrell was to direct a second company at the New. This company came to be known as 'Waiting for Larry'.

Before going into details about this company, which was to include Edith, here is an incident illustrating in what small regard she was then held by some people on the periphery of the theatrical profession.

The Old Vic management wanted photographs of Edith for the front of the house, and as she had none in her possession, I went to H. M. Tennent's press representative to ask if she would kindly lend us some.

The Press Office was at the back of the dress circle bar in the Apollo Theatre, and having learnt from Alec always to carry a torch in the theatre, I was able to light myself up the unlit stairs, where I met and lighted Miss Muriel St Clare Byrne, a Shakespearian scholar and lecturer and one of the leading members of the Society for Theatre Research. She was on a similar errand, needing photographs of Edith for one of the Society's publications.

The press representative, who was sitting behind a large desk but offered chairs to neither of us, was extremely uncivil, saying that Dame Edith was nothing to do with H. M. Tennent and that she had no photographs, although Edith had played almost exclusively for the Tennent management before the war.

Some years later when Edith was once more playing for H. M. Tennent in a number of highly successful plays, it was a very different matter, with this representative frequently requesting interviews. But even then she disliked approaching Edith through her secretary.

The first part which Edith was engaged to play in the new Old Vic company, was Lady Wishfort in Congreve's *The Way of the World*, the play in which she made such a great success as Millamant in Sir Nigel Playfair's production in 1924. James Agate wrote of that performance: '. . . this face, at such moments, is like a city in illumination, and when it is withdrawn leaves a glow behind.'

In the new production Faith Brook played Millamant, and I am sure she would agree that she was not ready for it. With Edith in the same play, reviving memories of her former triumph, and achieving a further triumph as Lady Wishfort: 'My face is like an old peeled wall', it cannot have been easy for her.

T. C. Worsley wrote in the *New Statesman*: '. . . it would take a young actress of the first quality to stand up to Dame Edith Evans as Lady Wishfort.' And Harold Hobson wrote: 'When Dame Edith played Millamant my great predecessor wrote that she was "like a city in illumination". Well, that was twenty-four years ago, and the lights are still shining.'

But apart from Edith and several other experienced players, the company was young and untried. T. C. Worsley's notice had included this criticism:

The rest of the cast (Mr Robert Eddison as Witwould must be excepted) seemed to be clumsily adopting some fancy-dress idiom to match their fancy-dress clothes, and were hopelessly at odds with both. They reduce the subtle brilliant rhythms to a sort of English film version of the 18th-century diction. But when Dame Edith Evans speaks, the words cascade and check, pause and then gush, straight from a living person who has always, you are convinced, spoken just so.

Edith felt as T. C. Worsley did about the importance of rhythm, likening it to a ball game with the players tossing the ball back and forth; if a player muffed his catch or dropped it, the rhythm was shattered. An example of perfect rhythm was when Edith and John Gielgud played together in the thirties; they tossed the ball back and forth with practised expertise, creating a perfect symphony of sound.

The other part which Edith was engaged to play was Madame Ranevsky in *The Cherry Orchard*, directed by Hugh Hunt. I have seen many Madame Ranevskys, including Dame Peggy Ashcroft and Gwen Ffrangcon-Davies, but none to equal Edith.

Again T. C. Worsley: 'Above all, there is Dame Edith Evans. More than any other Madame Ranevsky I have seen does she bring with her the whole of the part of this feckless, emotionally self-indulgent and warm creature.'

Harold Hobson commented in his book *Theatre 2*: 'Cedric Hardwicke told me the other day that Dame Edith Evans was born to play Madame Ranevsky, and she brought to her tonight a radiance as brilliant as that of high summer, yet tinged with a sweet autumnal sadness.'

So Edith had a great personal triumph, but better teamwork was needed to make the season a success. John Burrell, who had directed *The Way of the World* had an intellectual approach, giving the company pages of notes after each rehearsal, but he lacked the imagination to inspire young players.

It was not an atmosphere in which Edith could be happy. There are some actors who prefer playing with companies in which their star shines more brightly by comparison, but this was not Edith's way. Again using the simile of a ball game, she said that an actor, like a tennis player, could only play his best game with players of his own class. This lack of class put Edith in the position of a guest-star with a repertory company, but she had never played with a repertory company and had no desire to start now. She was unfailingly patient and uncomplaining, never discussing with me until months later her dislike of this engagement, but she must have felt desperately frustrated.

She was also lonely, and to employ a pet expression of hers, she lacked 'a chum'. The younger members of the company were admiring, respectful, but not chummy. It never occurred to Edith that they might be shy. 'Why should they be?' she would have asked. 'I'm not an ogre.' She was not, but she too was shy, too shy to make the initial approach. The barriers remained up.

On the last night she sat waiting in her dressing-room for a taxi, surrounded by cushions and make-up box, and the moiré silk eiderdown in a case which Katherine Cornell had given her in America, and which she always used for her rest after the matinée. The other members of the company were calling goodbye to each other in the passage, laughing and joking, but no one came to say goodbye to Edith. She waited there, sadly disregarded, with only myself to wait with her.

Chapter Eleven

Daphne Laureola was written by the doctor-playwright James Bridie, whose real name was Osborne Henry Mavor, and who had already written a number of successful plays including *Tobias and the Angel* and *A Sleeping Clergyman*. But none had the triumphant impact of *Daphne*, owing to Edith's superb performance.

A great deal has been written as to how Edith came to play the part of Lady Pitts, some of it inaccurate. The reason was that after James Bridie's death in 1951, Winifred Bannister, who was planning to write of his work, wrote to Edith suggesting a meeting but not suggesting that Edith might be too busy to see her.

Edith took offence. She told me to write and say that it was not convenient for her to give an interview, so the book did not have Edith's co-operation, and Mrs Bannister's account of how *Daphne* came to be produced was not altogether accurate.

It was generally supposed that James Bridie wrote the part of Lady Pitts for Edith, but that was not so. In the winter of 1948 a rumour went the rounds of the theatre that the part had been offered to almost every leading actress in London and New York, all of whom had turned it down. Edith, who had a great respect and affection for Bridie, asked to see a copy of the play. She read it, liked it, but was not unduly enthusiastic. I read it and was wildly enthusiastic.

The play was certainly unusual, but its poetic use of words was exhilarating, and the part of Lady Pitts was a challenge to any actress, though only a great actress could play it successfully. If

Edith played it, it was the stuff of which Midnight Matinées were made. I am not sure whether Midnight Matinées exist today, but at that time it was usual to have one if a player was giving a particularly memorable performance, so that fellow-artists who were working could have the chance to see the play.

When I told Edith how I felt, she accused me of being over-dramatic, but she had already decided to play Lady Pitts. When Bridie heard the news he sent her a telegram with the words 'Nunc Dimittis'. It is not doing Edith an injustice to say that she hoped that having played Lady Pitts, Bridie would write her another and better part. Many years later she was to play in Robert Bolt's *Gentle Jack* for the same reason.

Daphne Laureola was to be presented by Laurence Olivier, who had formed his own company, Laurence Olivier Productions. He had no great faith in the play, but was anxious to present Edith whom he greatly admired. This lack of faith persisted throughout the rehearsal period, though not among the players who fortunately knew nothing of it, and there was a certain amount of cheese-paring over the sets which were designed by Roger Furse. He told me later that in the first act, which took place in a restaurant called Le Toit Aux Porcs, part of the flooring was of a very temporary nature as everyone was sure that it would not be needed for long.

There was no cheese-paring over Edith's dresses which were by Molyneux, and were absolutely glorious. They were given to her when the play ended, and there is a press photograph of her wearing a particularly glamorous champagne-coloured satin dress, receiving George VI and Queen Elizabeth when they attended the charity première of the film *Odette*.

Murray Macdonald was to direct *Daphne*. He and Edith were old friends and he had directed her and Owen Nares in *Robert's Wife* in 1937. Edith had also worked with him in the war when he ran the Garrison Theatre in Salisbury.

Peter Finch was to play the young man Ernest Piaste. Laurence Olivier had 'discovered' him during the Old Vic tour of Australia, and this was to be his first appearance in England. There was also Felix Aylmer as Edith's husband Sir Joseph Pitts.

The atmosphere at rehearsal was happy from the start, the reverse of the Old Vic engagement. There was an absence of friction, and Edith learnt her lines with unaccustomed ease. Although the speeches were long they were rich and lyrical, and Edith broke them up so skilfully that they are remembered to this day by the heads of her profession.

They were remembered by Michael Redgrave in his book *The Actor's Ways and Means*, when he wrote: 'Few among the thousands who saw this actress [in *Daphne Laureola*] realise that the magic of that performance was largely the magic of verbal control, the understanding and manipulation of words. We talk of her personality, her magnetism, her wonderful assumption of beauty, all of which she has in abundance. They are so compelling that the audience does not analyse the result.'

Daphne opened at Wyndham's Theatre in March 1949. It opened cold, without a prior-to-London tour, as the management's lack of faith led them to believe that provincial audiences would not find the play attractive, and provincial critics would kill it with bad notices before it had a chance to reach London.

But word of Edith's performance had travelled round theatrical London, and sitting in the stalls on the first night I could feel the atmosphere charged with excitement. I too was excited, but also apprehensive. I felt that this unusual play would be either a triumph or a disaster. There could be no middle course.

As everyone knows who was lucky enough to be there that night, it was a triumph. When Edith came on at the end of the play to take her call in a glorious long black dress, the house rose to her, cheering and applauding. She stood there for a moment, then dropped into an elegant low curtsey. She said later, that when she came on she had no thought of curtseying, but quite involuntarily found that was what she was doing. It was the ultimate triumph of a triumphant evening, and one that she carried through until the end of the run.

My old friends in the gallery had been wildly enthusiastic, and the alley-way outside the stage door was jammed solid. Edith had to be smuggled out to a car at the front of the house, while I took another car to carry home the mass of flowers, presents and telegrams. I had ordered all the newspapers to be delivered to Albany next morning, and sat at the foot of Edith's bed reading her the highlights of the notices; there were a great many. But the most attractive notice was written later by T. C. Worsley for the *New Statesman*:

What a pleasure and a delight are the intervals in a play that is a crackling success from the start! And how this reflects itself at once in the high edge on the chatter, the confident nods between acquaintances at the bar, the exciting re-telling of this or that particularly memorable stroke! Such was our happy experience last night at Wyndham's Theatre . . . with Edith Evans displaying a mastery of her medium, an assurance and a variety that are unmatched on the stage today . . . She is now at the very height of her powers.

There were other splendid notices, particularly Harold Hobson's in the *Sunday Times*: 'Bridie is sustained by Dame Edith's shattering performance, upon which, for brilliance, I believe the very constellations will look down with jealousy. Every smile is like the rising of the sun, and every syllable she speaks a song.' And Sir Beverley Baxter wrote in the *Evening Standard*: 'I think this is the best acting Edith Evans has ever done, but her triumph is aided in many delicate ways by a young Australian actor, Peter Finch, who plays Apollo.'

On the second night Queen Mary, an indefatigable patron of the theatre, was in the stage box. Edith's dark days were over.

Chapter Twelve

During the run of *Daphne Laureola* I had a better opportunity than ever before to study Edith's approach to her work. She had learnt her job with the famous Vedrenne and Eadie management at the old Royalty Theatre in Dean Street, where her great friends were Mary Jerrold and her husband Hubert Harben whose clear speech was an inspiration to her. It was an age when strict discipline in the theatre was accepted as a matter of course, and when christian names were not bandied about. When Dame Irene Vanbrugh died in 1949, and Edith spoke an appreciation of her on the radio, she told her listeners how much she had been respected, so much so that her fellow-actors always addressed her as Miss Irene.

Edith still enforced a strict discipline on herself, and expected it from any company with which she played. I remember her wrath one hot summer day on seeing a young member of the company sucking an ice cream cornet in the prompt corner.

All the rules of the theatre had to be observed. I have already written of Winifred's gaffe of waiting in Edith's dressing-room during the performance and the same applied to me, I had to be out half-an-hour before the curtain rose. But I sometimes managed a few minutes' grace. It was then that I witnessed a transformation which I shall never forget.

When Edith was made up and dressed, she would sit very still, only her hands moving over and over in her lap, while she shed Edith Evans like a skin and Lady Pitts took over. It was a miraculous transformation and her dresser and I would sit as if mesmerised,

Graphic Photo Union

Receiving honorary degrees: (*left*) at London University, 1950, and (*below*) at Cambridge, 1951. Dame Edith received further honorary degrees from Oxford, 1954, and Hull, 1968

London News Agency

With George VI and Queen Elizabeth at the première of the film *Odette*, 6 June 1950

as indeed we were; to have spoken would have been an outrage. When I told Edith how we felt she said that Guy had felt the same, that when he sat with her in her dressing-room she was a stranger to him. He too never spoke.

This identification with her part worried Winifred, who said, quite seriously, that she was afraid that as Lady Pitts was a dipsomaniac, Edith might take to drink. She never did, but she knew instinctively how Lady Pitts would have behaved.

What I am writing about Edith may apply to any great actress, I had no chance to judge, but I should imagine that Edith's sensitivity was something above the average; watching her face when she was annoyed one could see the nerves fluttering under the pale, almost transparent skin. What caused her extreme annoyance, if not anger, was not to be warned of any change which she might encounter on the stage, such as an actress with a new hair-style, or even a different colour nail varnish, or an actor with a different colour tie. This could, and did, upset her, making her pull up short and fluff her lines.

Despite her sensitivity Edith never lost her down-to-earth realism, and a copy of the night's takings was brought to her dressing-room each night; she also kept a strict watch on the timing of the play – if it over-ran she had to know the reason why. The reason was usually because someone had lost control of the audience, allowing it to laugh too long and get out of hand.

Edith's audience control was remarkable. I think she looked on them as a lot of children who had to be kept kindly but firmly in order, and unlike Dame Sybil Thorndike who loved her audience, Edith kept hers at a distance.

One night I was watching the play with a perceptive friend who said: 'I always feel that she's saying, "don't get too close to me; don't touch me".'

In this Edith was not unique. In his book *Eleanor – Portrait of a Farjeon*, Denys Blakelock wrote of how Miss Farjeon, explaining the exceptional reserve of a fellow-writer, said: 'I understand her. She doesn't want to be *fingered*.' It was a description which fitted Edith perfectly, not only in the theatre but in her off-stage life. As well as not wishing to be 'fingered' she held strong views on not meeting dramatic critics socially. She thought it wrong, and once entering a lift and seeing W. A. Darlington, drama critic of the *Daily Telegraph*, she gave a cry of dismay and almost threw herself out before the doors closed.

She believed in retaining the magic of the theatre, and how could there be magic if player and public were all jolly good fellows together? On the first night of *Daphne* the press representative brought a crowd of reporters into her dressing-room. She was shocked and angry. Her dressing-room was her workroom and they had no right to violate her privacy.

If this sounds grim and inhuman, a certain aloofness was necessary to Edith if she was to do her best work. Each day was a build-up to the evening performance; each night was a first night. She may not have been 'chummy' with her audience, but she never let them down.

Among other factors necessary for Edith to do good work was a happy relationship between herself and her dresser, something which applies to all star actors as anyone who reads theatrical memoirs knows. In Richard Aldrich's *Gertrude Lawrence as 'Mrs A'*, he mentions her dresser Boxie (Mrs Boxall) who had dressed her in the past, and dressed her again when Gertrude Lawrence returned to England in 1948 to play in Daphne du Maurier's *September Tide*. Boxie (to us she was Doris) dressed Edith in *Waters of the Moon* in 1951, and was one of the many splendid dressers who included Katie, Gladys, and Diggie, all of whom contributed enormously to Edith's well-being in the theatre. But in 1949 relationships were not so happy. The Tennent management, for whom Edith had played before the war, had almost a monopoly of first-class dressers, but Laurence Olivier Productions had no regular dressers. They engaged Joyce.

Joyce was an ebullient creature with no knowledge of dressing, except of dressing herself, and Edith would come off the stage to find Joyce sitting at her dressing-table trying out a new hair-style. Joyce also had a highly dramatic personal life, and every evening some fresh drama had erupted since the night before. Although a good-natured girl, the highly-charged atmosphere that she generated was not what Edith wanted in her dressing-room. 'If there has to be drama,' said Edith, 'I'm the actress!' So Joyce left and Gladys came.

Gladys was Gladys Viddecombe, formerly Wardrobe Mistress with the Fol de Rols, and eventually with the National Theatre at the Old Vic. She was an extremely capable, but at that time very shy woman, and the idea of dressing Edith terrified her.

The chief terror concerned the champagne-coloured satin evening dress. When 'Overture and Beginners, please' had been called and the actors had assembled on stage for the first act, the call girl would knock on Edith's door with: 'Your call, Dame Edith.' The dresser, who would be Gladys, then picked up the hem of the very long dress and went with Edith on to the stage, arranging the folds of the dress after she had sat down.

Gladys confided in me her terror of going on the stage and perhaps not arranging the dress to Edith's satisfaction, but in the event she did it beautifully, as she did everything. She was the best of dressers and the sweetest of women.

Another duty for the dresser was to stand at the side of the stage with a glass of water, ready for when Edith came off and needed a drink for what was always a dry mouth.

When in 1965 she played the part of Mrs Forrest in Enid Bagnold's *The Chinese Prime Minister*, a part in which she was not happy, glasses of water were secreted all over the stage so that she could take a sip whenever she felt the need.

I once performed this glass of water duty at the Coliseum where Edith was appearing in a Sunday charity performance. I was almost as scared as Gladys as the Coliseum had a revolving stage, and at any moment I expected to be facing the audience, clutching a glass of water.

The run of *Daphne* was marked by a number of supper parties in Albany. Edith's housekeeper Miss B, of whom more later, had left, but Mrs Janes, known to us as Jinny Janes, came in to provide delicious food.

Mr Polly, then the head of Jackson's wine department, introduced Jinny Janes to us. At that time Jackson's supplied cooks and other staff for dinner parties, and Jinny Janes was on their books. She came over from Battersea where she lived to work miracles in the tiny Albany kitchen, a kitchen so narrow that it was impossible for two to pass. Miss B had complained that she could not cook this and that because the stove was too small, but Jinny Janes would pile the stove with saucepans that appeared to reach the ceiling, whilst delicious sauces, soufflés, and zabaglione, were produced with great good humour and a lot of chit-chat between Jinny Janes and myself. There was an evening when Ruth Gordon and her husband Garson Kanin came to supper, and Miss Gordon smoked throughout the meal, as Americans often do. I inwardly wept on Jinny Janes's behalf at the waste of so much dedicated effort.

But there were other parties where Jinny Janes received her full due of appreciation. There was a buffet supper when I filled the bath with ice from the fishmonger to cool the champagne, and where the guests included John Gielgud, and Joseph Verner Reed, a millionaire American who, in the thirties, had lost some of those millions in show-business and wrote an entertaining book about it called *The Curtain Falls*. Another guest was Lady Allenby – Mary, Viscountess Allenby – with whom Edith was sharing a country cottage at Hothfield in Kent, as a solution to her weekend problem. Lady Allenby was an expert on Jersey cows, which conjures up a picture of a large woman in tweeds and corduroy breeches. Nothing could have been further from the truth. She was a tiny, pretty, very feminine woman.

The association was not altogether a success. Edith wanted someone to look after her and 'cosy her' at the weekends, but Lady Allenby's concern was to make a home for her son Michael then, I think, still at Sandhurst. As she worked very hard at her job, a professional job not an amateur interest, she was in bed and asleep when Edith arrived home late on Saturday night. There was no delicious little meal waiting for her, no gossip while she unwound after a week of Lady Pitts. In a way they were too much alike, neither of them was a woman's woman.

There was an incident during this time at Hothfield which I shall always remember. It had nothing to do with cosiness or bowls of hot soup, instead it had to do with snow – drifts of it.

During the winter of *Daphne*, a young driver from the local garage, his name was Horace, would come up to the theatre on Saturday evening to drive Edith home to the country for the weekend. The particular evening which I remember so well came at the end of a week of atrocious weather – snow, ice, thaw, then snow again. No one in their senses would have taken out a car, certainly not after dark, and Horace must have waited, as I had once waited, for a telephone call cancelling the trip. But no call came, if Edith could drive through falling bombs Horace could certainly drive through falling snow, and so he came up as usual. He came up safely, but the return journey was not so fortunate.

The road to Hothfield ran over Wrotham Hill, a long climb with a steep gradient, and a tricky descent at the other end. But it was negotiated sucessfully until, at the foot of the hill, disaster struck; the car stuck fast in a snowdrift. The road was deserted, there was no help at hand, nothing to do but spend the night in the car with no heating. But Edith did not appear to have been disturbed, and when daylight came she and Horace set off over the frozen snow to the nearest garage and the means of pulling Chloe out of the drift. Where others would have dramatised the story Edith treated it as a lark, then let it drop; she disliked people who 'went on' about things.

I have strayed from the subject of supper parties, but there were two very important personages who never came to supper in Albany. I am speaking of Laurence Olivier and Vivien Leigh, at this time the uncrowned King and Queen of Theatreland, who in 1949 invited Edith to one of their weekend parties at their country home, Notley Abbey. These weekends were very grand affairs, starting on arrival, after two Saturday performances and a considerable car drive, with a full-dress dinner party. The visit progressed on the same high note of grandeur until Monday morning, and to someone like Edith who prized simplicity, particularly in the country, the finishing touches must have been breasted with relief.

This royal hospitality called for a reciprocal show on Edith's part. She could not invite the Oliviers to her little shared cottage at Hothfield, but there was Jinny Janes and her superb cooking in Albany. Edith talked about a supper party, talked about it at length, but nothing came of it. Why was that? It may sound absurd, but Edith was, in many ways, an extremely shy woman, and the idea of entertaining the Oliviers frankly terrified her. She could not live up to their standards, or so she thought.

Murray Macdonald, who directed *Daphne*, was a close friend of the Oliviers, and they must have discussed with him the fact that Edith never invited them to supper. They were hurt and bewildered; it seemed to them a strange way to behave. Murray was too tactful to mention this to Edith, but time and time again he begged me to encourage her to ask them. She never did, and the Oliviers never crossed the threshold of Albany.

Daphne was still running when *The Queen of Spades* was about to be premièred, and two large publicity women from the film company came to Albany to arrange for Edith's personal appearance. They were most surprised to learn that she was in a play: they had never heard of *Daphne*, and I doubt if they knew that Edith was a stage actress. But if she was, and they took my word for it, could not her understudy go on? She could not. They were deeply incensed.

These ladies were not alone in having strange ideas about the theatre. Edith's bank manager, a charming man, most helpful to me when I started my job, once asked what Dame Edith was doing. When I told him that she was rehearsing he was amazed. 'But surely Dame Edith doesn't rehearse!' he exclaimed, and I gathered that he thought she took her place in the play when the others had finished rehearsing among themselves.

Both *The Queen of Spades* and *The Last Days of Dolwyn* were shown within a few weeks of each other, and although neither was a commercial success, both were triumphs for Edith. Two films and a play, three completely contrasting character studies. There was hardly a newspaper or magazine without a picture of Edith.

A particularly charming montage appeared in the *Sketch*, then a glossy magazine like the *Tatler*. As well as publishing the montage they presented Edith with a delightful little silver statuette as best actress of the year. I was not so delighted with the statuette which was full of nooks and crannies and almost impossible to clean.

A well-known daily newspaper also gave Edith an award as best actress, and Edith gave the money to charity. Another award that, according to rumour, Edith was to receive, was the Ellen Terry award, also for the best actress of the year. But somehow it never materialised and the award was never heard of again.

Readers of newspapers and magazines may have been familiar with Edith's face but not so the box office staff. One morning she decided to attend an understudy rehearsal, and instead of entering the theatre by the stage door she came in through the front of the house. She was half way up the stairs when the box office manager, not recognising her, called to her to come down. As she did not come down he bustled out of his box to be met by an amused Edith who told him who she was, and pointing to the box office queue said: 'If it wasn't for me you wouldn't be selling all those tickets!' Poor man! But like cloakroom attendants, box office staff have little opportunity to see the play.

George VI and Queen Elizabeth came to the play. The King was recovering from his first illness, and rather than climb the stairs to the royal box they sat in the front of the stalls. They enjoyed the play, but afterwards the King said to Edith: 'She wasn't a very nice woman, was she?'

The next time that Edith met the King was at a Royal Academy dinner at Burlington House where a loan exhibition was on show. Edith sat next to the King, and later showed me her menu card on which he had drawn a child's version of a cat to illustrate how little he knew of art.

All kinds of people enjoyed *Daphne*, including my Uncle Walter, a dear but not an intellectual. After that, if people told Edith they feared they might not understand the play, she would say: 'Of course you will, Jean's Uncle Walter did.'

The play ran successfully into 1950, when something occurred, it must have been the General Election of that February, that caused the figures to slump. Had *Daphne* been presented by an established management such as H. M. Tennent, they could have ridden the slump and the play would have returned to full houses. But Laurence Olivier Productions had just suffered a disastrous setback with a monumental flop at the Duchess Theatre and had no resources to carry *Daphne*. The play closed.

During its run Christopher Fry had been to see the play, and the following morning he rang Edith to say that lying in the bath he had thought of an idea for a play for her. It was a rash remark to make to a non-writer. Edith expected the script to be in her hands within a few months. But Christopher Fry was a slow worker, and an idea did not necessarily mean that he was ready to sit down and begin. Edith rang him monthly and yearly asking when she could expect to read the script, but it was 1954 before *The Dark Is Light Enough* was produced.

Chapter Thirteen

Edith did not have to wait for Christopher's play before starting work again. During the run of *Daphne*, Leyland Hayward, the American impresario, had been to see the play, and there was talk of taking the production to New York, but before this happened the British Council invited Edith to carry out a poetry reading engagement on the continent.

In 1950 these British Council tours were the only way of enjoying a continental holiday, the official travel allowance being so small as to be almost useless. Lectures tours, poetry tours, and all other kinds of cultural tours were much sought after, though in Edith's case it turned out to be not so much a holiday as grinding, uncomfortable work.

Before she left she tried out her programme on audiences in the North of England, where on one occasion I forgot to pack her evening shoes, and Edith had to appear in her glamorous black Molyneux dress, once the property of Lady Pitts, wearing a pair of sensible brogues.

She also tried out the programme on a few friends in Albany; Winifred Oughton and myself, and Susan Holmes, a friend and secretary to Dame Sybil Thorndike and Dame Lilian Braithwaite. It was the first time I heard Edith read poetry as opposed to Shakespearian verse and I was disappointed. Edith was not an ideal poetry reader and I found later that I was not alone in thinking so. In the reading of humorous and satirical verse she was unrivalled, but with more serious poetry her voice was too individual, her approach too large: she swamped the verse.

But in this particular instance Edith was not entirely to blame. The British Council is an intellectual organisation and the poems were selected by scholars and intellectuals, with no thought as to whether they were suited to the reader. As Edith had a great respect, even awe, for scholarship, she never questioned their choice. Neither did her friends. We sat like dummies, applauding politely, though I was surprised that the forthright Winifred did not speak out. But it was better so; Edith appeared to be satisfied.

After a lapse of years I cannot recall the exact mechanics of the tour nor all the cities Edith visited. At one time I kept a diary in which I recorded not only facts and dates, but momentary irritations and dislikes without time for reflection. The result was that the black became blacker than black and the white whiter than white. After a while I gave up the diary and destroyed it.

I had always sent a copy to Dodie, but when I asked for its return she refused, quoting 'emotion recollected in tranquillity'. Of course she was right, but it would be useful to me now.

However, I can recall that Edith stayed either in hotels or at the Embassy, but on one occasion she stayed in a private house which she described in a letter as appallingly uncomfortable. What sparked off this diatribe was the fact that she had been given a boiled egg for breakfast, not in an egg-cup but in a napkin ring. She never forgot this, it was shoddy housekeeping. It may also have been that that particular city had never heard of egg-cups.

Edith's annoyance was aggravated by her feeling unwell and suffering from a streaming cold. A photograph taken at the time shows her standing with her hosts, looking like a woman who might die at any moment.

So most of her letters, apart from the egg-cup incident, were about her cold, her hoarseness, her difficulty in speaking; nothing about her audiences. But there were a few personal touches such as her letter from the British Embassy in Lisbon, in which she thanked me for my 'beautiful packing', so I cannot have forgotten any evening shoes. And in another letter from Barcelona she thanked me for being kind to Gwen. It had also been a pleasure. Gwen and Marda Vanne had given up their home in Pretoria and returned to England, where I met them at Waterloo Station with a car and a trailer for their mountain of luggage. It was my first meeting with Gwen since my days with Dodie (Gwen and Dodie were old friends) and as I came to know her better my affection and admiration grew. She was the most unselfish woman I ever met.

In an earlier letter from Madrid, Edith had told me that the American tour of *Daphne* had been settled, and rehearsals for this was what she returned to. Unfortunately it was not to be the same company which had played at Wyndham's. Laurence Olivier had persuaded Peter Finch to appear for him in another play, telling him it would be better for his career than going to New York with *Daphne*. This was a blow to Edith who had enjoyed playing with him, and during the run of the play had gone down to the theatre in the mornings to take him through the classics.

Now a young Dutch actor, John Van Dreelan, was engaged to play Ernest Piaste. He may have rated as a star in Holland, but in England he would have figured in a minor constellation. He appeared not to know his strength and Edith accused him of bruising her arms every time he touched her. He was certainly good-looking but the day of matineé idols was over.

The other change in the cast was Cecil Parker taking over from Felix Aylmer. Cecil Parker was a gifted actor. He was also devoted to his wife whom he liked to have travelling with him as he said she kept him from going off the rails. One morning after a night with the boys, he shamefacedly told Edith that it would never have happened if Muriel had been there. But charming as he was, and he was very charming, he was not suited to Sir Joseph Pitts as Felix Aylmer had been.

There was a short provincial tour before the company flew to New York. In Manchester, Bridie came away from the Opera House chuckling: 'It's a good play! A very good play!'

And so it was, but this production did not do it justice. Leland Hayward came to a performance and was horrified. It was too late to cancel the American venture, but his gloom and despondency was all too apparent. Everyone, with the possible exception of John Van Dreelan, knew the play was doomed.

Daphne opened at the Music Box Theatre in New York to bad notices (although Edith's performance was praised) and it closed after fifty-six performances, leaving her free to fly home to speak the Prologue at the reopening of the Old Vic in the Waterloo Road.

Olive Harding drove me to the airport to meet her at five o'clock on a bleak Sunday morning, where we arrived to find a large car

74

from the Old Vic, filled with large young men with large ther-
moses of coffee. They too had come to meet Edith, but when she
landed she was tired and not in the mood for making the effort of
talking to strangers. So she drove back with Olive of whom she was
extremely fond, and the young men were left with only the doubtful
pleasure of driving me home.

It was one of those thoughtless acts which were apt to make
Edith unpopular. Had she been told that the young men were hurt
she would have been surprised; it never occurred to her.

But all must have been forgiven when, on 17 November, to quote
Sir Beverley Baxter:

The curtains parted and our favourite Dame pronounced the first
line: 'London be glad! Your Shakespeare's home again.' Whereupon
the audience cheered, which was just as well, for the lady's lips were
trembling and she was fighting back the tears. Then like a good
trouper she pulled herself together and went through Mr Hassall's
prologue to its final line: 'Dear friends, dear Poet, welcome home
again', with only such falterings and fluffings as enchanced the matter.
In short, it was an unforgettable beginning to an unforgettable
occasion.

Chapter Fourteen

While Edith was in New York I forwarded a letter from London University saying that they had voted to confer on her the Honorary Degree of Doctor of Literature, and asking her to reply to the toast of 'The Guests' at the dinner before the encaenia. This was Edith's first academic honour – there were to be three more – and she was particularly pleased at its coming from her home University, London. She was proud of being a Londoner born and bred, not a Welshwoman as so many people believed.

When the day came for the encaenia I did not remind her that she was replying to the toast. It was not that I forgot, but at that time she disliked being reminded as much as she disliked being questioned. It was foolish of me, as although she never made notes for a speech, she did make points in general conversation which were later incorporated in her speech. It was a form of trying it out on the dog which was easily recognisable, but there had been nothing of the sort this time and I should have been warned.

Edith never blamed me for this lapse, but the shock of discovering what she had to do, only a short while before she had to do it, and in the presence of Sir Norman Birkett KC, who was also receiving a Doctorate, must have been immense. But the late Dame Lillian Penson, the Vice-Chancellor of the University, told me that Edith made a splendid speech.

Edith had a points table for speeches – very good, good, get by. At one dinner, sitting next to the Bishop of London, he asked how she could make a speech without first having a drink. This remark scandalised Edith as it would have scandalised the late Nancy, Lady Astor. 'A man of God,' she would have said, 'should not have to rely on the bottle for inspiration.'

It was during the encaenia that I received the first warning of a nervous breakdown. It went unrecognised at the time.

For too long I had been working too hard, in fact, since Edith's housekeeper Miss B had left, something for which I was largely responsible and for which I am still deeply ashamed. She was a lady from a county family who clung rigidly to her rights. She had had virtually three months' holiday while Edith was in South Africa, but on the Sunday following Edith's return she took her day off as usual, leaving Edith's bed unmade, the fire unlaid in the sitting-room and no coal in the bucket. She would have got on well with Cheveral, one of Dodie's housekeepers who had worked for Lady Cynthia Asquith at Stanway. One Sunday when Dodie complained that her bed was badly made, Cheveral retorted that 'even real ladies don't have their beds made on Sunday'.

Miss B had other grievances, one being that she did not eat with Edith in the dining-room; instead she lunched later alone. It was an arrangement which Edith said, had she been the housekeeper, she would have preferred. But on the verge of hysteria one lunchtime, Miss B rushed into the room carrying her plate, sat down at the table, and without a word of explanation started to eat.

She understood neither Edith nor the theatre. She once told me that Emlyn Williams had telephoned: 'And he called himself Mr Williams. Wasn't that a funny thing for an actor to do?' She was also quite remarkably genteel, and would return from the butcher saying that she had asked for 'a nice piece of steak for two ladies'.

Miss B would have made an ideal companion-housekeeper living as one of the family, for another grievance was that she was not asked into the sitting-room for a chat and a cigarette, although she knew of Edith's aversion to cigarettes.

She was getting on our nerves, but I should have made an effort to understand her point of view, which was that it was degrading to earn her living as a working-housekeeper. Instead I persuaded Edith to let me take over the housekeeping, but as Potter was no longer there I also took over the washing and ironing. All this as well as being a secretary. The result was that I bolstered my flagging energies by consuming about half a bottle of sherry each day.

77

What happened at the encaenia was what might have been expected in the circumstances. On the evening in question I had several glasses of the aforementioned sherry, a hot bath, and after showing off my Fortnum and Mason finery to my fellow-slaves on the top floor, and wearing a heavy Kolinsky fur coat, too large and too long for me, I drove off in a taxi.

It was a cold night and I went into the assembly hall still wearing the coat, and sat down beside Angela Baddeley and her husband Glen Byam Shaw, who were also Edith's guests. The hall was an interior structure with no windows and a very efficient heating system. In no time at all I was sweating under the awful coat, and as the procession started to file in I felt myself going weak at the knees as if my legs had turned to water. My head was bursting, my hands were clammy; I was terrified of disgracing Edith by fainting.

All I wanted was to get out of the hall, but we were sitting in the middle of a row, packed like sardines. I had to stay, and for what seemed hours, and was certainly a long time, I sat with clenched fists, willing myself not to fall flat on my face. I survived. As we left the hall the symptoms vanished.

Having been reduced to a state of panic I remember little of the ceremony, but I have a photograph taken at the time, which just to look at is a pleasure. In the background, sitting at a desk, is Dr Ivor Evans, Principal of Queen Mary College and the Public Orator; he was also Vice Chairman of the Arts Council, a great lover of the theatre and admirer of Edith. He is smiling broadly, evidently delighted with what is going on, and what is going on is that Edith, wearing her academic gown over Lady Pitts's black dress, is kneeling before the Earl of Athlone, then Chancellor of the University, after he has conferred the degree. He is clasping her hands, and they are smiling happily at each other.

But although I recall so little of the ceremony, I must have had some lucid moments, for I remember Sir Norman Birkett making a charming and witty speech without resort to notes.

At the time I blamed my condition on the hot bath, followed by the cold night air, followed by a session in the over-heated hall wearing the ridiculous coat. But from then on the symptoms came and went, though never so alarmingly. Perhaps a feeling of dizziness in the theatre or the cinema. There was some time to go before I finally collapsed.

It was after the encaenia that Edith played the part of Lady B. in the film of *The Importance of Being Earnest*. Edith played Lady B., as she called her, in every medium – stage, radio, television, gramophone recordings, film. After that she had had Lady B. and refused to play her again.

In the film, which was directed by Anthony Asquith, Michael Redgrave played John Worthing, while Joan Greenwood played Gwendolen and Dorothy Tutin played Cecily. But it never compared with the pre-war matinées at the Globe Theatre, when John Gielgud played John Worthing, and first Jean Cadell and later Margaret Rutherford played Miss Prism, with Gwen Ffrangcon-Davies as Gwendolen and Angela Baddeley as Cicely. Edith told me that when she and John Gielgud played the handbag scene, leading up to the lines: '. . . that reminds one of the worst excesses of the French Revolution, and I presume you know what *that* unfortunate movement led to', they had the greatest difficulty not to giggle.

The Importance of Being Earnest was first shown at the Odeon, Leicester Square, in 1951, and I went to the première with Winifred. We went to all Edith's premières together as Edith was always playing in the theatre and gave us her tickets. On this particular evening Gilbert Harding was sitting behind us, very noisy and very much the worse for drink. He declared in a loud voice that all he wanted to see was Edith Evans in the handbag scene. He saw her, guffawed loudly, then left.

Chapter Fifteen

N. C. Hunter, who died in 1971, was much abused by the critics for being a popular playwright; popular being a derisory term for the type of theatre that a high proportion of people enjoyed. Praise was only praiseworthy when applied to plays with a message, plays which made their audience feel guilty rather than jolly. Young critics such as Kenneth Tynan were naturally in the vanguard, but many of the older critics, fearful of being considered *vieux jeu*, brought out their scalpels. This post-war cult of the obscure, later to become a kind of religion, drove such fine playwrights as Noel Coward and Terence Rattigan temporarily from the theatre.

But even pre-war there had been a small band of critics, headed by James Agate, who disliked what were then called drawing-room comedies', and sighed after better things. Dodie once sent him a Christmas card depicting a flock of sheep, shepherded by a winged angel, on which she had written 'Mr Agate in search of an author'. He was right to advocate more serious plays, but he overlooked the number of people who went to the play simply for relaxation.

Another aspect of the popular play which infuriated some critics, was that players of the first class should waste their talents on such light stuff. In 1937 many critics had objected to Edith appearing in St John Ervine's *Robert's Wife*, a play they considered unworthy of her, but which ran for 606 performances at the Globe Theatre, giving pleasure to thousands, including myself. In the same way they had objected to John Gielgud wasting his talents in Dodie's *Dear Octopus*, which ran for 376 performances at the Queen's Theatre and would have run longer had it not been for the outbreak of the Second World War.

Now N. C. Hunter's *Waters of the Moon* was presented by Binkie Beaumont, Managing Director of H. M. Tennent, with a galaxy of stars, including two Dames, Edith Evans and Sybil Thorndike, Wendy Hiller and Kathleen Harrison, and such fine supporting players as Cyril Raymond and Nan Munro.

The critics gnashed their teeth, and after the first night T. C. Worsley wrote:

Our regrets about *Waters of the Moon* is of another kind. It is that visitors this summer will not see our incomparable Edith Evans in a play worthy of her. This is a sad piece of irresponsibility on the part of the theatre. *Waters of the Moon* will, all the same, find a large public, the public which so enjoyed Miss Dodie Smith's plays before the war, though they may find this a little slow and a shade too long (whenever Dame Edith is off-stage) . . . the author has added to the formula some rather crude borrowings from the Russians, but his play remains essentially a cosy middle-brow, middle-class piece, inhabited by characters by no means unfamiliar in brave old Theatreland; which anyhow gives everyone a chance to play their own selves without bothering about acting.

This was unjust to N. C. Hunter. His plays may not have carried a profound message, but they carried a warm human message about people. He also wrote extremely actable parts, as did Dodie, which was why so many star players consented to play them. Edith suffered no qualms of conscience in agreeing to play Helen Lancaster; she had no feeling of letting down herself or her public.

Frith Banbury was to direct *Waters of the Moon*, and came to Albany to discuss the play with Edith. He was a painstaking director who had gone back to the grass roots, and gave the life history of each character as he understood it. It took hours to explain and was wasted energy. Edith was polite but bored; her instinct would tell her all that she needed to know about Helen Lancaster.

In interviews to the press, and on radio and television, Edith often spoke of her approach to a part. Of how she started tentatively, not yet sure of what she meant to do, of how she experimented and threw away, adding a little here and there, until suddenly, one day, the character was born. This meant that her director must trust and not hurry her.

The part of Helen Lancaster was appallingly difficult to learn, long and full of non-sequiturs, and I would suggest little tricks for helping her to remember her lines. Hearing words can be an exhausting business if one puts one's heart into it, and I did put my heart into it night after night, and often in the morning if Edith had time to spare. Eventually it proved the last straw that toppled me over into a nervous breakdown.

My domestic duties had slackened, otherwise I should have toppled sooner. Mrs Wheeler, known as Tilly, had taken Potter's place. Like her she lived in Palmerston Road, Kilburn, and had known Edith in the past. But she lacked Potter's sense of dedication. She had little affection for Edith, I suspect she found her rather silly. Tilly had her own ideas as to how middle-aged women should behave, and being an actress was no excuse for excessive temperament and sensibility.

Appreciating Edith as an actress was essential to working for her. Throughout our long association, if I felt particularly anti-Edith, I would take myself to a play or film in which she was appearing, and watch with delight this amazing woman who bore no resemblance to the woman I knew in Albany. Every scrap of ill-feeling would be washed away and I would return home ready for any sacrifice on the altar of such a magnificent actress.

At this time I was not suffering from ill-feeling but from nervous exhaustion. The crisis occurred one Saturday morning when Edith was going down by train to Hothfield, and I went out to buy the ticket from a travel agent in Regent Street. Leaving Albany I felt perfectly all right, but as I crossed the end of Sackville Street everything started going round in circles and my legs almost gave way. At that time there was a hoarding between Sackville Street and Swallow Street, hiding some bomb damage not yet repaired. The hoarding had an immense advertisement for a detergent called Tide, and as I stood there trying to regain my self-control, three women who might have been office cleaners passed by. I can see them and the hoarding quite clearly today.

After a few minutes I managed to stagger into Regent Street and buy the ticket, but returning along Piccadilly the dizziness started again and I had to take a taxi the last few yards to Albany. As I stepped out of the taxi the dizziness vanished, as it had at London University. A few minutes later, as I was reaching up for

Edith's suitcase in a high cupboard, it was back again worse than before.

All hope of hanging on until Edith left for the station had to be abandoned while I sat in the sitting-room sipping brandy and trying not to pass out. After a while I was able to go upstairs and lie on my bed, and Edith, who had been extremely sympathetic, was able to go to Hothfield. Before leaving she asked one of the housekeepers to keep an eye on me, which she omitted to do.

I lay there until Monday morning when Tilly, with whom I got on well, came and made me a cup of tea. When Edith returned she was highly displeased at finding me still lying there: sustained sympathy did not come easily to her, particularly sympathy for someone who could disrupt her work. But she relented to the extent of bringing me two huge doorsteps of very stale bread and butter.

The next morning I got up, and still feeling shaky went downstairs, though any idea of venturing into the street terrified me. Eventually I managed a walk along Piccadilly, and coming back saw Edith looking out for me in the rope walk. This uncharacteristic concern for my welfare moved me deeply.

So for yet a little while longer we were back to a surface normality. Fortunately there was no question of my attending rehearsals. An edict had gone forth that no one, absolutely no one except the cast, was allowed into rehearsals. This was to prevent Dame Sybil's husband, Sir Lewis Casson, from coming along and giving Dame Sybil direction contrary to Frith. Sir Lewis had been a forceful director and was still a forceful old gentleman who could cause friction.

I was only too pleased to stay in Albany, and when Edith left for rehearsal in the old Stoll Theatre in Kingsway, I would retire to my little room and stay there until it was time to go downstairs and prepare Edith's supper as a prelude to hearing the interminable words.

The words were a nightmare to us both, but thankfully we won through. What sustained me was the belief that once Edith was launched in her part and the word-hearing sessions were over, I would return to normal.

The play was to open at the Theatre Royal, Brighton, and we travelled down by train on the Sunday morning. At Victoria Station we had to wait at the barrier for our train to come in, and as my legs felt like jelly I kept walking to and fro, trying to steady them. Edith must have thought I was mad; I probably was.

Most of the company, including ourselves, were booked-in at the Royal Crescent Hotel, an hotel much frequented by theatricals to whom it gave special terms, and to whose difficult hours it catered sympathetically. Until Ivor Novello died in 1951 he had a permanent suite there. On this particular Sunday the restaurant was crowded, and as we took our seats, and as the heat and noise enveloped me, I knew I had come to the end of the road.

If I looked as I felt, I looked like a frightened rabbit, but like a rabbit I nibbled nervously through my lunch and drank my after-luncheon coffee in the lounge where Edith chatted to her friend Willie Armstrong, at one time Director of the Liverpool Repertory Company. When she left for a word rehearsal at the theatre I fled to the sanctuary of my bedroom.

That evening there was to be a dress rehearsal to which I had been looking forward, but even Pongo could not have dragged me out of that bedroom, let alone the hotel. I stayed there until the morning, then knocked on the door of Edith's adjoining room and told her that I could go on no longer and was ordering a car to take me to Eastbourne where my mother was living.

I was letting Edith down when she needed me most: there would be flowers, telegrams, letters after the Brighton first night, but anyone who has suffered a nervous breakdown knows that moment of capitulation. Edith was wonderfully understanding, as she so often was in a crisis, and both of us were sure that I would be back in a few days, certainly before the London first night. We were wrong. Having capitulated my collapse was total. I lay in bed for weeks, looked after by my mother, without whom I would have been packed off to a mental home.

Chapter Sixteen

It was all too apparent that my career as Edith's secretary was over, and at that time I am sure she had no intention of having me back. As far as her own career was concerned Edith was completely ruthless, anyone and everything that might injure it was out. A secretary addicted to nervous breakdowns was a liability, and as such I too was out. She engaged another secretary, Olive Harding's younger sister Mrs Butler, who like Edith's former secretary Peggy was not dedicated to the job. I suspect that Olive pushed her into it, but Mrs Butler found the job had at least one peculiar facet – any secretary of Dame Edith must be prepared to put her hand in her pocket.

The reason for this may sound silly, but it was understandable to anyone who knew Edith and her preoccupation with finance. The trouble was that she had never done her own household shopping, her idea of food prices was pre-First World War. So when I, and later Mrs Butler, returned from Brewer Street and showed the bill to Edith, she would launch into a tirade on exorbitant prices and her inability to pay them and still live in Albany. She would then sidetrack on to her wages bill, though in my case I was earning less than I had with Dodie in the thirties; a labourer was only worthy of his hire if he did not have a private income.

All this was boring and time-wasting and did not show Edith at her best, so in pursuance of a quiet life, I would take off the odd shilling and sixpence when telling her the price, making up for the difference out of my own pocket. At the time I blamed myself for being chicken-hearted, but when I met Mrs Butler she told me that she had employed the same subterfuge, and not being well-off, and having two children and a policeman husband whose wage was not excessive, she found the drain on her resources more than she could manage. Making ill-health the excuse she gave in her notice.

It is only fair to say that had Edith known that her secretaries found this subterfuge necessary she would have been horrified. She would also have thought us extremely silly, as no doubt we were. In October she wrote me a particularly charming letter asking if I felt well enough to come back. I was overjoyed.

I had become bored with the life of a seaside town, however comfortable mother made it. When one has lived for years with an outsize personality, ordinary people appear dull and uninteresting. The excitement and the drama are an essential way of life. The nervous breakdowns, the resentments, the cooking of the accounts, are a small price to pay.

So I came back to Albany, but not to live. During my absence Mr Stone had engaged a nurse and she had taken over my room, while Edith had converted her own housekeeper's room into an office. So I found a large furnished room, dark and inhospitable, in Culford Gardens behind Peter Jones. The rent included breakfast which was brought up by a manservant wearing a white coat, but the coffee was lukewarm and I suspected the toast of having been made the night before. So I left and moved to Gloucester Place where I had lived for a short while after leaving George Street and going to Albany, and where I was looked after with loving care and was extremely happy.

But I was not happy in my work. I knew I was suspect, as are all sufferers from nervous breakdowns, with or without the stigma of a mental home. It was understandable – normal people do not break down.

To illustrate this point: on Friday mornings I went to the offices of Edith's agents in St James's Street to collect her weekly salary cheque, as she liked me to pay it into the bank on a Friday. Sometimes I had to wait, but Olive never invited me to wait in her office, and I was left sitting on a hard chair in the outer office. I knew the reason, that she did not wish to be involved with such a difficult character, and I sympathised with her, but it did not help morale.

The cheque which I went to collect was substantial as *Waters of the*

Moon was playing to packed houses and was to do so for over two years. A long run is boring for the actors but a blessing for their staff who are free every evening, and as Edith rested in her dressing-room after the matinée I was free for most of Wednesday and Saturday.

But if I looked forward to matinée days, Edith did not. As everyone knows, Dame Sybil was much beloved by her public, and on matinée days was visited by Women's Guilds, Unions, and Institutes. These ladies would bustle up and down the stairs to Dame Sybil's first-floor dressing-room, passing Edith's dressing-room on stage level and invariably using her lavatory, which strangely was also the Royal Box lavatory, and was situated opposite her door. This would have disturbed anyone, but to Edith with her dislike of sharing, it was an outrage.

This was not the only cross which Edith had to bear. Dame Sybil's behaviour in her part was a cause of real distress to Edith. In his book *Lewis and Sybil*, their son John Casson wrote: 'Sybil has always been an apparently guileless and innocent-looking scene-stealer whatever the size of her part', but he omitted to mention that Dame Sybil would sit and wink at the audience while Edith was playing a scene. I saw her do it and was horrified; to Edith, a dedicated professional, it was unforgivable.

John Casson went on to say: 'When she knitted quietly on the sofa you had to watch her because knitting suddenly became to you the most important thing in the world', but it was an occupation where grimacing could be as effective as winking. Again: '. . . and when anyone was doing anything Sybil had only to blow her nose for everyone else to become the background to it'. Dame Marie Tempest had used the same gambit, waving a large chiffon handkerchief to draw the audience's attention away from her fellow-players. This did not endear her to the other members of the company.

There was little social life to record at this time. Occasional supper parties, but when Edith was playing she seldom accepted daytime engagements. Like Dame Marie Tempest she always rested in the afternoon so that she came fresh for the evening performance.

I can recall only one exception to this rule during the run of the play – a Centenary Matinée in honour of William Poel, the Shakespearian producer and scholar, which took place at the Old Vic in July 1952.

Edith was chairman of the organising committee. She always called Poel 'my old master', and he had come to a performance of the Streatham Shakespeare Players, founded by Edith's old elocution teacher Miss Nell Massey. There he had seen Edith and asked her to come and act for him, and for the Elizabethan Stage Society whose plays he produced. This led to her playing Cressida in *Troilus and Cressida* at the King's Hall, Covent Garden, in 1912, and from that moment exchanging the role of milliner for that of professional actress.

During the Old Vic performance I was standing at the side of the stalls with Miss Muriel St Clare Byrne, a Shakespearian scholar on the committee of the Society for Theatre Research who had helped organise the Matinée. She was also a friend of Dorothy Sayers, creator of Lord Peter Wimsey, and had collaborated with her in writing the play *Busman's Honeymoon* which was produced at the Comedy Theatre in 1936.

Miss Byrne's admiration for Edith was unbounded, and as Edith was now on the stage reminiscing about Poel, doing it very wittily and causing a great deal of laughter among the audience, Miss Byrne became very excited, positively jumping up and down. 'She's got them!' she cried. 'They're with her all the way! She's hitting a boundary every time!'

It was not only her afternoons which Edith kept inviolate; as Millamant had kept her 'closet inviolate' so Edith kept her Sundays, the only free day in the week of a working actor. But as was the case with the Centenary Matinée there had to be an exception, this time the annual performance at Smallhythe in Kent which took place on or about the anniversary of Ellen Terry's death. The performance was given in the large thatched barn which Ellen Terry's daughter Edith Craig had converted into a theatre, and there before an invited audience the leading members of the theatrical profession spoke their pieces. For most of the performers it was something of 'a chore', but they gallantly carried on as long as the old ladies who lived there, and had known Ellen Terry, were alive.

On the particular occasion of which I am writing the performance was covered for the *Theatre World* by someone calling herself Looker-On. I say 'herself' as the notice was somewhat catty, giving the impression that the writer was perhaps an unsuccessful actress making the most of her opportunity to flex her claws at the expense of more successful members of the profession. She wrote that 'Athene Seyler appeared as a somewhat roguish Queen Elizabeth', and that 'Dame Edith Evans gave a rather artificial reading of two of the Sonnets'. This may have been true, I was not present, but coming from an outsider it made my blood boil. I cannot remember Edith appearing again at Smallhythe; perhaps it was the last anniversary performance.

As the months, and then the years passed, Edith became increasingly wearied of Helen Lancaster. Some star players have a clause in their contract limiting their appearance to a certain length of time, but Binkie Beaumont had always refused this to Edith, a compliment she could have done without. But now, to give her a fresh interest, he had Helen Lancaster re-dressed by Balmain. She had previously been dressed by Hardy Amies.

Hardy Amies was Edith's personal dressmaker since Edward Molyneux had closed his salon in Grosvenor Street; both men enjoyed dressing Edith, who had a splendid figure and wore their clothes with style. I once went with her to a fitting at Molyneux and was absolutely fascinated, particularly by the old-English butler who welcomed us in, and the huge floor-to-ceiling mirrors which accentuated one's imperfections. Everone was charming, from Captain Molyneux's sister, Mrs Lumley, who ran the salon, to Edith's vendeuse, Mrs Miller, both of them highly sophisticated and witty women. While I was there an over-dressed little dumpling of a woman came in, weighed down with jewellery so that she looked like a Christmas tree. 'Oh, no!' I said to myself, 'she could never be dressed by Molyneux.' But Molyneux had his own way of dealing with such situations. Mrs Miller went up to her, and in the nicest possible way told her that they had so many orders on hand that they were unable to take any more. The little dumpling left quite happily and no one's feelings were hurt.

Edith was sorry to leave Molyneux but Hardy Amies was an equally distinguished dressmaker. Edith approved his use of the old-fashioned word 'dressmaker' as she approved his choice of words when driving back with him after a lunch date he told the chauffeur to 'drive to the shop'.

It was imaginative of Binkie to think of re-dressing Helen Lancaster, but then he had a great understanding of women and the way to handle them. On two later occasions when Edith was appearing under different management and things went terribly wrong, I am sure Binkie could have put matters right.

So *Waters of the Moon* went on its way through 835 performances. But no play runs for ever, except perhaps *The Mousetrap*, and at last Edith was free. She celebrated her freedom by taking a holiday at St Tropez with her friend Muriel Adams.

Chapter Seventeen

Christopher Fry had at last finished *The Dark Is Light Enough*. When he sent what he considered to be the final draft to Peter Brook, who was to direct, asking him to pass it on to Edith, Peter Brook told him that he could not possibly expect Edith to read it in its present state. What that state was I cannot imagine, as when the script finally arrived in Albany the revisions were still written on scraps of paper and the backs of old envelopes.

James Bridie once said that Christopher Fry was a reincarnation of Shakespeare. It was when we were in Manchester with *Daphne*, and Bridie was in an expansive mood, but at that time Christopher Fry was a highly successful poet and dramatist, having written such plays as *The Lady's Not for Burning*, *Venus Observed*, and *A Sleep of Prisoners*. Later his popularity waned, particularly with young people who preferred T. S. Eliot, and he turned to writing film scripts.

Christopher Fry was not one of my favourite playwrights and I rather dreaded his first nights. After a day as Edith's secretary his plays were too much like hard work, needing too much concentration. I would sit with my usual first night friend, herself having done a hard day's work, both of us tensed to breaking point, knowing that if we relaxed for a moment we were irretrievably lost. The exception was an extremely witty play *Ring round the Moon*, a translation from the French of Jean Anouilh. Expecting to be exhausted, we were exhilarated.

Unfortunately *The Dark Is Light Enough* was not exhilarating. The verse was certainly beautiful and Edith, in the part of the Countess

Rosmarin, spoke it beautifully, but not all the casting was so happy.

Of course there were some fine performances, particularly by Hugh Griffith, and by Peter Barkworth as the Countess's son Stefan, but James Donald was miscast in the important part of Richard Gettner. The Countess's daughter Gilda was played by Margaret Johnston, a first-class actress but one whose superb memory caused Edith great concern. Miss Johnston was word-perfect in every part including her own, and if anyone paused for a moment she was in like a flash, prompting madly, and would have been quite capable of carrying on the play single-handed.

And of course there was Peter Brook, then aged twenty-nine, and not renowned for tact. Edith made her first entrance down a flight of stairs, and there is no need to stress that her timing was impeccable, but Mr Brook told her to count five before starting to come down. Edith was indignant. 'What does he think they pay me for?' she asked.

There was a long tour prior to London, with one change of cast, and as Edith was not happy I went up to the Adelphi Hotel in Liverpool, and later to the Royal Crescent at Brighton, to be with her. Although she had no deep affection for me, having me around seemed to help, perhaps because I had the familiarity of a household object which can be soothing.

During my time with both Dodie and Edith I acquired an encyclopedic knowledge of the principal station hotels of our great cities. The Queen's at Leeds, the Caledonian in Edinburgh, the Midland in Manchester, the Queen's at Birmingham, the Adelphi in Liverpool. They all charged five star prices, but the Adelphi had one redeeming feature, its tea. It was a gargantuan meal, with trollies laden with muffins, crumpets, sandwiches and scones, cakes and pastries. If one worked one's way through it was impossible to eat dinner, and in the interests of economy it was even possible to forego supper after the show. Other economies could be practised. Christopher Fry and his friends took their after-luncheon coffee at a nearby Lyons rather than pay the Adelphi's high prices.

The Dark Is Light Enough opened on 30 April 1954, at the Aldwych, then a shabby and unfashionable theatre. Looking back, it is clear that Binkie Beaumont, who was presenting the play, had little faith in it. But he was an astute man of the theatre and if Edith, one of his most valuable assets, wished to appear in a play by a prestigious poet, he could afford to be generous. Magnanimity could pay dividends later.

The notices for the play were not bad but neither were they, in the main, enthusiastic. Anthony Cookman of *The Times* wrote:

The theatrical impact is a little uncertain. Though Mr Fry has subdued his poetic imagery to the tone of what he describes as a Winter Story and his wit nearly always earns its keep, there are, in effect, still too many words ... Dame Edith Evans plays the Countess impeccably, ravishingly ... Not perhaps a major play but an immensely interesting one.

Sir Beverley Baxter in the *Evening Standard* found more to enthuse about when he wrote: 'There is no other living dramatist with such a command of the English language. His verse-prose makes the dialogue of ordinary plays shrivel like raisins ... you have language surging to an orchestral climax. You will hear English spoken by a distinguished cast. You will see dignity and importance restored to the West End theatre.'

During the run of the play Edith was off for a couple of nights with a bad throat and her understudy took over. Because Edith was such a healthy creature no one troubled much about an understudy, the only time she had been off in years was during the war when she fell off a hay cart at Washenden at harvest-time. During the run of *Daphne* she had fallen in Leicester Square on her way to the theatre, but though bruised and shaken she carried on with her part. So there was now no suitable understudy, only a little woman, a capable actress, but as unlike Edith as could be. A doctor friend of mine, to whom I had spoken enthusiastically about Edith, went on one of these nights and was bitterly disappointed. Something like that does no good to a play and from then on a first-class understudy was provided.

It was now time for Edith to receive her third Doctorate, her second had been in 1951 when she received an Hon.Litt.D. of Cambridge Unversity, now this was to be an Hon.D.Litt. from Oxford University. As the encaenia was on a matinée day the theatre was closed for the afternoon.

This Oxford encaenia was the first time that anyone met Judith Wilson who was to become so important in Edith's life.

Judith, who was a cousin of the first Lord Rothermere, had been a fan of Edith's since the days of Millamant. From time to time she would send Edith a cheque for a hundred pounds, asking her to do with it as she thought best, and Edith either gave the money to a theatrical charity, or in one instance to a theatrical friend who was having a difficult time. She never spent the money on herself, though we learnt later that was what Judith had intended; instead I sent careful accounts showing where every penny had gone.

Edith liked the way Judith expressed herself in her letters, and thought it would be nice to send her a ticket for the Oxford encaenia, the other ticket going to Olive Harding. Olive sat next to Judith in the Senate House and Edith and I were anxious to know what she was like. Olive told us that she was small, very pretty, and beautifully dressed, wearing pearls which looked real. They were.

That night, after the evening performance, Edith gave a party on the stage, the centre-piece of the buffet being a Jeroboam of champagne. This was a souvenir of *Waters of the Moon*. There was a line in the play when Wendy Hiller mentioned Perrier-Jouet 1943, and each Christmas during the run of the play the firm in question sent bottles of champange to the cast, the Jeroboams being reserved for the stars.

Edith had asked me to take the Jeroboam down to the theatre early so that the caterers could put it on ice, but I forgot to take it down until the party was due to start. Edith was justifiably furious, but as the Jeroboam had been kept in Albany's underground cellars it was still remarkably icy.

Edith did not need champagne to spark off her high spirits: she was the only person I ever met who could become drunk on sheer enjoyment. She loved a party, preferably a theatrical one; smart society and lionising she abhorred. She told me that after her success as Millamant the society hostesses of the day, the lion-hunters, tried to take her up, but she politely refused their invitations, preferring to go her own way in her own milieu.

On this particular night she was at her best, gay and ebullient. I always thought she had a lot in common with Gracie Fields, both larger than life personalities, and I am sure that if Edith had not been a stage star she might have been equally starry on the Halls.

But not all her ebullience could keep *The Dark Is Light Enough* running. Not long after the night of the party the play closed.

Chapter Eighteen

In 1955 Edith was sixty-seven and had been on the professional stage for forty-two years, and since her triumph as Millamant in *The Way of the World* in 1924 she had been one of the heads of her profession.

This was not a comfortable eminence to maintain, particularly in the years between the wars, the years of the star system, when the star was of supreme importance and the play came a poor second. Even after the Second World War the system was still operative; in 1949 the director Peter Coates wrote a book entitled *No Star Nonsense* in which he lambasted the star system, saying: 'The present-day commercial managements are far more interested in vehicles for stars than in plays of ideas.'

This was very much the case in the thirties when I first began putting down stools in the Gallery queue. Nine a.m. was usually early enough to secure a good seat, but if the play starred Edith Evans or John Gielgud it was a case of six a.m. or earlier, and I was always in a panic until I reached the theatre and had staked my claim. On at least two occasions, unconnected with Edith or John Gielgud, I was there at midnight, once at Drury Lane for an Ivor Novello first night, and again at His Majesty's for Noel Coward's *Operette*. We unashamedly went to see our particular stars, and had they played a small part in a team-effort it would have been deeply resented.

This attitude, which was not confined to the Gallery, put a great strain on the stars. It meant that Edith must be particularly careful in her choice of a play and her part within the play; not for her the light-hearted acceptance of a part because it meant good money. She had to wait for a part which was, even if it sounds pompous, worthy of her talents; she must never, never let her audience down. This choice of a part became increasingly hazardous as Edith grew older. One well-known comedy actress told her that she wished she had never been raised to the status of a star, as instead of being continuously in work she was now out of work for long periods.

Edith was seldom out of work except in the unhappy period after the Second World War. For most of her working life, she was appearing in play after play for eight performances a week, always as star or co-star. This could prove exhausting and however long the run of a play Edith never allowed herself to relax. She could be downright angry with players who came to the theatre after a successful first night as if no further effort was required of them. There were some actors in the first rank who would give a magnificent performance on the first night, never again to equal it: one of these was Godfrey Tearle, but as at least one of the others is still with us I will mention no further names. To Edith every night was a first night.

Not all stars lived in this rarefied atmosphere. When Dame Sybil Thorndike was playing in *Treasure Hunt*, a play in which she spent some time in a closed sedan chair, she spent that time learning her lines for a new play, and on radio I heard Athene Seyler say that during the run of a play at the Criterion Theatre she sat on the stage totting-up her household accounts in her head. Edith could not have behaved in this way, it would have been against her nature to slip casually in and out of a part. Like the boy on the burning deck she would have remained in character with or without the benefit of an audience.

But today the boy on the burning deck is treated as a joke, and perhaps Edith would have done well to take her work more lightly, although by so doing it is doubtful whether she would have attained the heights she did. But given her natural temperament and the pressures under which she worked, multiplied by the years in which she had been on the stage, is it any wonder that she sometimes cracked?

It can happen to the most unlikely people: Dame Margaret Rutherford for instance. Until I read her autobiography as told to

Two views of Gatehouse

Relaxing on stage, 1959 (*l. to r. in front*): Charles Laughton, Leslie Caron, Angela Baddeley, Mary Ure, Dame Edith, Harry Andrews, Laurence Olivier; (*behind*): Peter Hall, Paul Robeson, Glen Byam Shaw

Roger Wood

Miss Gwen Robyns, I would have thought Dame Margaret able to shake off any pressures. Her account reveals the contrary:

All through my acting career I have suffered from over-strain and breakdowns. It is not the least uncommon in the theatre world where we actors walk a tightrope between nervous and physical exhaustion and live in a mixed world of fantasy and reality . . . For some actresses the cure is a change of part. For me it is periods in a nursing home where I can have complete rest and find myself again. Sometimes I bounce back quickly, other times I feel whacked and wonder if I shall ever be able to act again. Shall I ever be able to make that nightly entrance, to remember my lines, to keep my technique fresh and credible?

So if Dame Margaret and others as distinguished could crack, why not Edith? And she did.

Chapter Nineteen

André Roussin's play *Nina*, had had a great success in Paris in 1949–50, where it ran for over 400 performances with Mme Elvira Popesco playing Nina. Binkie Beaumont had seen it, recognised it as a vehicle for Edith, and commissioned a translation. This translation arrived in Albany while Edith and Muriel Adams were on holiday in Paris, and as I had been given permission to read the script, I did. I liked it immediately.

I was as enthusiastic as I had been over *Daphne*. It was very French, a *ménage à trois*, and in every word I could hear Edith speaking. I was sure that she would have a triumph, another Midnight Matinée, and had everything gone smoothly I still think that I was right. The question of age was unimportant: Nina was a middle-aged woman whose lover was beginning to tire of her.

When I met Edith and Muriel at the airport on their return from Paris I could talk of nothing but *Nina*.

Binkie, and Muriel who had herself seen the play, were equally enthusiastic; so in a lesser degree was Olive Harding. Edith was not. She felt instinctively that the part was wrong for her, but allowed herself to be persuaded against her better judgement. Bernard Shaw had said that in a part in which she did not believe, she was not worth a penny to the management. In this case he was proved right.

Nina ran into difficulties from the start. There was the casting: there were only two supporting parts – husband and lover; it was absolutely essential that they be right. The first choice for the lover was Charles Goldner, but he was already ill when he read the part and died in hospital a week later. After that actors of various nationalities were approached, including Anton Walbrook and Francis Lederer, but they were either found unsuitable or were unwilling to play second fiddle to Edith.

Eventually James Hayter was engaged to play the husband, a good actor but not a sex-symbol, and the lover was to be played by David Hutcheson, too young for Edith and lacking the necessary authority. He knew it, and was as unhappy in his part as Edith was in hers. Rex Harrison was to direct.

Even before rehearsals started Edith was showing signs of strain, the strain of embarking upon a venture for which she had no enthusiasm, rather an active dislike. She wilted; that was the only word for it. She was like a flower which had stood 'too long i' the sun', which loses its colour, whose head droops, and whom no one can recognise for the splendid bloom it was.

The part of Nina was not difficult to learn. Every evening in Albany Edith knew her words perfectly, every morning at rehearsal at the Haymarket Theatre they had flown.

I had never before sat in on a rehearsal of one of Edith's plays, but now she made the unprecedented suggestion that Judith Wilson and I should attend a rehearsal of *Nina*.

Since Judith's appearance at Oxford she and Edith had become friends. Judith's mother had died, and when Judith was staying at Brighton, at the Royal Crescent, she invited Edith to join her for a weekend. The visit was a success. Later they went on a winter holiday to Montreux.

I was with them at the airport when Edith noticed Ursula Jeans and her husband Roger Livesey, both looking very professional in their ski kit and carrying their skis. Edith was fond of them both, and rushing across asked if they were going to Montreux. They were not, but to one of the smaller resorts frequented by ski enthusiasts. 'Oh, how I wish I were going with you!' exclaimed Edith.

Judith's composure remained unshaken, but I was distressed on her behalf that Edith should be so hurtful. She had no intention of being hurtful, she was simply nervous and apprehensive at the idea of spending a fortnight with someone whom she knew so slightly.

She need not have worried. Judith was a remarkable woman in every way, a fact which Edith came to appreciate. Alone of Edith's friends who had read *Nina*, Judith did not approve, and what we saw at rehearsal only went to harden her disapproval.

Edith started without her book, and I knew she knew her lines, but within a matter of seconds she had worked herself into a frenzy, almost in tears because she was unable to remember a word. James Hayter and David Hutcheson looked thoroughly miserable, and when it came to their turn it was obvious that they were hopelessly miscast.

Rex Harrison sat in the stalls wearing a huge camel-hair coat and chatting to Kay Kendall. He had the script on a drawing-board, propped against the seat in front of him, but as far as I can remember he never consulted it, and throughout the whole rehearsal I cannot remember him making a single suggestion. He probably realised there was nothing he could do, short of getting up on the stage and playing both male parts himself.

Judith was horrified, as well she might be, but I was still so besotted by the play that I rudely disagreed with all she said, insisting that it would be all right on the night.

That was the first and last rehearsal of *Nina* that I attended, but several times I took Edith's lunch to the theatre, and we would sit together in the royal box while she ate. I think she was so utterly miserable that even walking home to lunch was more than she could face.

Everything continued to be against *Nina*, including a rail strike. Olive Harding, an excellent driver, offered to drive Edith and me up to Liverpool for the opening of the tour.

The journey started well enough, until driving up Park Lane, not then a one-way street, Olive remembered that she had forgotten to bring a spare pair of spectacles – she had a variety of these all with different coloured rims to match her clothes – so we had to go out of our way to fetch them.

Then Edith, sitting in front with Olive, started to slump so low in her seat that she could have been dead, unconscious, or just sleeping. At the hotel where we stopped for lunch we met Jack Hawkins, which temporarily cheered her, but as the journey continued she slumped lower every mile.

Olive and I were deeply concerned, and were not helped by having to communicate in whispers. Of the scenery *en route* I remember nothing, except for a little town with a castle on a hill where we stopped to buy a packet of glucose sweets; we needed the energy. Then on again towards the Mersey tunnel. When we were in the tunnel, at the best of times a macabre experience, it was made more macabre by the fact that Edith had not spoken for miles. We could have been carrying a corpse to the mortuary.

It was with a feeling of deep thankfulness that we emerged into the daylight and drove the short distance to the Adelphi Hotel. As we got out of the car I breathed a prayer that never again would I be obliged to make such a journey. My prayer went unanswered.

That night we dined in the restaurant, and to prove that I am not over-dramatising the wilting flower motif, when the head waiter, who had known Edith for years, showed us to a table, he did so without recognising her. I wanted to jog his memory so that Edith should have the best attention, but realising my intention she shook her head.

That was Saturday. When I went into Edith's bedroom on Sunday morning she told me she could not go on – the same words which I had used at Brighton.

By this time Binkie had arrived with M. André Roussin, to be met by the news that his star player was on the verge of a breakdown.

Although Edith was a Christian Scientist the terms of her contract required her to see a doctor, and at her request Binkie rang Sir Henry Cohen, later Lord Cohen of Birkenhead, a friend of Edith's and of all theatre people; he was Chairman of the Board of the Liverpool Repertory Theatre.

I have no idea what they said to each other, but Sir Henry must have seen that as long as *Nina* was hanging over Edith's head she would never improve. He and Olive had a lengthy conference in the bathroom, a strange place for a conference but it adjoined Edith's bedroom. Afterwards he told Binkie that in no circumstances was Edith to go on, certainly not that week in Liverpool, probably not for several weeks.

There was nothing Binkie could say. The understudy, this time a charming and talented actress, was warned to hold herself in readiness to go on. M. André Roussin's journey had not been necessary.

The remainder of the day I spent reading the Christian Science Lesson Sermon to Edith. 'Thank you, Jean,' she said, 'you read beautifully', a compliment that the one-time stammerer never forgot. When the reading was over I ran down the hill to the docks and the landing-stage, where I could breathe the sea air and watch the ferries, packed with happy, normal people, crossing to Wallasey and Birkenhead.

The question now was, where should Edith go to recuperate? She solved that problem herself. 'I want to go to Gwen. I want to go to Gwen,' she told us over and over again.

Gwen was a most loving and hospitable person. When I rang her at her cottage in Essex she said: 'Give Edith my love and tell her to come at once.'

As the railwaymen were still on strike I ordered a car, and the next day when everyone was lunching in the restaurant and there was no one to see us, we left.

The car turned out to be a rugged, utilitarian vehicle, capable of covering the distance but not in luxury. But anything was a Cinderella's coach that carried Edith away from Liverpool and *Nina*.

It was a slate-grey day and we drove through a slate-grey country, with now and again slate-grey workmen's cottages and slate-grey little towns and villages. How can I remember? Some things one never forgets.

Time came that we craved a cup of tea, but there were no cafés and no cottages offering teas to motorists. This part of the country was not interested in tea, or at least not in providing it for the public.

The pubs were closed, and though I banged on several doors no one would make us a pot of tea. At last I persuaded a friendly publican into making one, after explaining that Edith was the famous actress Dame Edith Evans, though at that moment she looked like a very old woman on the point of death. His family, who I am sure had never heard of Edith, brought out their autograph books. Everyone was charming. I was sorry to leave and drive off into the gathering dusk.

We passed through the outskirts of Cambridge and into the flat fen country of no hedgerows and unrelieved anonymity. It was now dark and Edith was the only one to know the way to Gwen's cottage on the borders of Suffolk and Essex. But Edith was no Ordnance Survey Map, and we were soon lost in a tangle of little lanes and by-roads. She was now on the verge of hysteria. The long drive, and now her vain attempt to find the cottage, were more than she could take. At one time she slipped to her knees on the floor of the car the better to peer from the windows. I feared that in desperation she might throw herself out.

And then there was the cottage with the lights shining out into the road, and there was Gwen at the gate, ready to welcome Edith with the warmth of her affection. It was wonderful to see Edith relax and to know that the journey was over.

There was no room for me to sleep in the cottage so I went to a near-by pub, and sitting in the lounge eating sandwiches and drinking strong coffee (I had given up sherry), I was the happiest woman in the world. I had shed my responsibilities, I was alone. It was a wonderful feeling.

After a couple of nights I returned to London, coming back to the cottage once or twice to see how Edith was getting on. She was getting on splendidly.

After staying with Gwen for several weeks she went to Judith at Codicote. I went down several times by bus, taking any important letters and staying the night.

Staying the night was Judith's idea; she felt Edith might be bored alone with just the two of them. She need not have worried – the house contained a television set.

This was Edith's introduction to television, rarer then than now and with only one channel. It became an instant passion, and Edith would sit through every programme however bad. It was a passion which never waned. In fact it grew, and when she and Judith acquired a country house and a television, Edith's viewing time spanned seven hours from five p.m. to midnight or whenever the stations closed down. When she was twitted over this her answer was that she liked to keep in touch, very much the same answer she had given for reading the left wing press.

So Edith was contented at Codicote and grew stronger, with Judith the perfect hostess and the house extremely comfortable, furnished with great good taste, and hung with Boudins, Guardis, and Augustus John drawings. There was also a large number of books reaching to the ceiling, and it was always a sadness to Judith that Edith took no interest in them; in fact when Judith and Edith moved to the country she treated them as something of a bore as Judith unpacked crate after crate – they took up so much space.

Judith's cousin, Cecil King, wrote in one of his books that Judith was plain and dull. She was not. She was exceedingly pretty and far from being dull she was well-read and witty, and above all she was a wonderful friend to Edith.

What were Edith's thoughts at this time, apart from her absorption in television? I had not the remotest idea. We all took it for granted that she would return to *Nina*, and presumably so did she: it was a serious matter to break a contract. Binkie certainly expected her to return to the play, otherwise he would not have carried on with the tour, however good the understudy. He was waiting for Edith, as the Old Vic had waited for Larry.

One of the towns in which the company was booked to play was Brighton, David Hutcheson's home town, after which his part would be taken over by Michael Hordern, and it was arranged that Edith should go down to Brighton and rehearse with him before rejoining the company.

Had Michael Hordern been engaged in the first place he might have saved the play, but now his inclusion in the cast came too late. But at the time the arrangement had Edith's approval and Judith and I went with her to the Royal Crescent Hotel.

On this occasion Edith had a suite, comprising sitting-room, bathroom, and two bedrooms. I had the spare room while Judith, in her undemanding way, slept upstairs. I remember washing my hair and drying it in front of the fire, while we all chatted and joked as though no one had a care in the world.

On the following morning Michael Hordern called to take Edith to the theatre, while Judith and I took the opportunity of riding on the open-top bus to Shoreham, planning to come back as far as Rottingdean. But half-way along the sea front we had a premonition that all was not well, and getting off the bus opposite the hotel we went up to Edith's suite.

All was certainly not well; voices were coming from the sitting-room. When we opened the door there was Edith looking pale and distraught, with Michael Hordern doing his best to calm her. It appeared that when they started rehearsing all the old horrors came crowding back. Michael Hordern had to return with her to the hotel. She was finished with *Nina*.

Olive had been sent for, as she always was when trouble was around, and when I met her in the hall she looked grim. As we went up the stairs she said: 'Does Dame Edith realise that if she refuses to play Nina it will mean the end of her career? No management would risk employing her again.'

I said that I understood, and later Edith said that she too understood, but it was impossible for her to play the part. Fortunately Olive was wrong. Edith's career was far from over.

As we boarded the London train we were like a party of children let out of school. We were all a little light-headed, and why not? We had finally buried *Nina*.

As a footnote to *Nina*, the play opened at the Haymarket Theatre in July of that year 1955, with Coral Browne playing Nina. The notices were unfavourable and it closed after 45 performances. But I still believe that if the casting had been right, and if Edith had believed in herself, she would have had a great success.

In 1974 I was to have this opinion endorsed by Harold Hobson of the *Sunday Times*, when he concluded a notice with the words: 'I shall always regret that years ago she abandoned the idea of playing André Roussin's inexcusable but strangely tender *Nina*, a play that has in it a speech which would have been one of Dame Edith's greatest triumphs, as in Paris it was one of Marie Bell's.'

However, in *The Theatre Now*, written by Harold Hobson and published in 1954, he writes: 'It was taken in translation to America in 1951, with Gloria Swanson in Mme Popesco's part of a middle-aged woman whose lover is beginning to tire of her. Miss Swanson soon tired of her, too, and during the preliminary run of the piece in Philadelphia, freely expressed her opinion that there was nothing in the character worth playing. Miss Swanson probably did find nothing in Nina, for in New York the play ran for only a week.'

Chapter Twenty

I am quite sure that Edith never took seriously the threat that her career was at an end, but the merciful demise of *Nina* left her thoughts free to return to the idea of a country home. In Kent, of course, with its memories of Guy and Washenden.

While at Washenden Edith had met Harold Nicolson and Vita Sackville-West who then lived at Sissinghurst Castle. Prior to *Nina* Vita Sackville-West had sent Edith a cutting and photographs from *Country Life* of a pre-Elizabethan manor house, originally a weaver's house, about twelve miles south of Tunbridge Wells. It looked delightful, but at that time Edith could not afford to buy it herself, and obviously it needed a staff and someone to look after them while she was working.

But she kept the cutting, and when Judith was thinking of giving up the house at Codicote and buying a flat in London (until then she had kept a room at the Hyde Park Hotel), she and Edith went down to Kent with the idea that they might share this country house which, as if it had been waiting for them, was still on the market. They fell in love with it.

The house was called Gatehouse, but as Edith prized her privacy only her close friends were to know the name or the locality. At one time Peter Wyngarde came to live opposite, and on a Sunday evening he knocked on the back door. Edith opened the door, and with a look of horror exclaimed: 'Oh, no!' It was not that she disliked Mr Wyngarde, she liked him very much, but she disliked the theatre intruding on her home. The 'Oh, no!' became a joke between them, but it illustrated Edith's feelings towards Gatehouse.

The house came up for auction and Judith sent someone to bid for her. The price she named fell short of the reserve, and as no one else wanted Gatehouse it was withdrawn. But Judith had not finished with it. Again she and Edith went down, this time to get an estimate for the repairs from Mr Barton, head of the firm of builders who looked after the structural repairs to Albany.

I went with them on a glorious summer's day with the house looking like a film-maker's dream and the grounds, though sorely in need of attention, beautifully laid-out and flanked with massive old trees and huge rhododendron bushes. But Captain Beale, who had come over from Sissinghurst Castle Farm, immediately raised objections, saying that such an old house would require a permanent maintenance man to see that the structure was kept in good repair.

There were other snags. Although the exterior was lovely the interior had obviously not been lived in for years. The kitchen quarters were in a particularly bad state with damp patches and even mould on the walls, and the hall looked like a great barn, and like a barn had bats hanging from the rafters.

Mr Barton was as discouraging as Captain Beale. No one had told him that Judith was an extremely wealthy woman, otherwise he might have looked at things differently and been more constructive. As it was he gave the thumbs down. Judith then called in a local firm who knew the house and had done work on it in the past. The repairs would be costly but not outrageously so. That was all Judith needed to know. She made an offer for Gatehouse which was accepted. It was theirs.

I say theirs, for they were to share all expenses, and until Judith was taken ill she kept the most meticulous accounts so that Edith need never feel beholden to her. In fact there were improvements that Judith could have made and did not, knowing that Edith would insist on paying her share which, at that time, might have been a burden.

This sensitive regard for Edith's feelings was one of Judith's most endearing traits. Once when they were attending a film première together and I asked her why she was not wearing some particular piece of jewellery (her jewellery, all from Cartier, was very lovely), her answer was: 'I couldn't wear that, it wouldn't be fair on Edith.'

Both Judith and Edith were so anxious to move into their new

home that they insisted on spending Christmas there in great discomfort among paint pots, ladders, and without a telephone. But
it was splendidly warm, with a new heating system and huge log
fires roaring up the chimney. There was also Judith's exquisite
furniture and pictures, and of course her books, and later when the
carpets were down and the deep-red velvet curtains were drawn in
the hall, it was the most beautiful house I ever saw.

During this time the *Nina* affair had faded into oblivion, so much
so that Binkie now asked Edith to play the part of Mrs St Maugham
in Enid Bagnold's play *The Chalk Garden*.

Enid Bagnold admired Edith greatly as an actress, and had always
wanted to write a play for her. Some years earlier she had sent her
the script of *The Chalk Garden,* badly typed with many alterations
which made it difficult to read, but worse still, it was impossible to
understand. No one could make anything of it.

It is a strange but true fact that authors, and this includes the most
distinguished, have an overwhelming urge to write plays. It could
be that whereas a book may reach only hundreds, a stage play reaches
thousands, and now with television it can reach millions. When I
met G. B. Stern she had talked at length of a play entitled *The Man
Who Pays the Piper* which had been a flop in 1931. It meant more to
her than all her successful novels.

Enid Bagnold was a distinguished writer with a unique command
of language, but her preference was for writing plays.

In her autobiography, Miss Bagnold told the history of *The Chalk
Garden*, and gave full credit to Irene Selznick for taking both her and
the play in hand, making it possible for it to be produced in October
1955 at the Ethel Barrymore Theatre in New York with Gladys
Cooper playing Mrs St Maugham. It was this version of the play
which Binkie was now to present in London if Edith would play
Mrs St Maugham.

I delighted in *The Chalk Garden* with its enchanting use of words,
but Judith always distrusted it, considering it pretentious. Edith
took a while to make up her mind to play Mrs St Maugham but
finally agreed. When later she played her in the film of the play,
shown in 1964, she was nominated best supporting actress by the
American National Film Board of Review.

John Gielgud was to direct, a choice which caused Edith some
initial unease. She was very fond of Johnny, as she called him, and

had great admiration for him as an actor but not as a director. She was disturbed by his habit of constantly changing his mind as to how the play should be presented. He would carry on for a week or more and then decide it would be better done some other way. He experimented endlessly, which was what Edith did with her own work, but was not a technique she encouraged in her director. At one time she had said that never again would she be directed by him, but now she relented, and as they were old friends, and as he understood and respected her approach to her work, it proved a happy association.

What was not so happy was Enid Bagnold's insistence on sitting-in on rehearsals, all day and every day, to ensure that none of her words were changed or omitted. But Edith had an instinct for words, saying that if she found a sentence difficult to speak the words must be wrong. She was usually proved right.

To a playwright every word is sacred, and to remove or alter one word is enough to bring the whole edifice crumbling. I recall a lengthy conference in Newcastle over the length of Dodie's *Dear Octopus*, which at that time ran for over four hours. Dodie was not comparable to Enid Bagnold as a writer but she was a more technically accomplished playwright, and ever word, which after hours of argument she consented to remove, was like drawing a tooth.

When *The Chalk Garden* eventually set out on its prior-to-London tour there was no need for me to go too. Edith was among friends; Peggy Ashcroft, who played Miss Madrigal, was an old chum to whom Edith was devoted, and there was also Felix Aylmer and Rachel Gurney. There was no fear of her feeling lonely or left out.

The play opened at the Haymarket Theatre on 11 April 1956. Judith and I were at the first night, and while Judith still had reservations, I was ecstatic. The pattern of the words was like a highly-coloured painting.

Kenneth Tynan, then drama critic of the *Observer*, wrote: 'On Wednesday night a wonder happened: the West End Theatre justified its existence . . . *The Chalk Garden* may well be the finest artificial comedy to have flowed from an English (as opposed to an Irish) pen since the death of Congreve.'

Anthony Cookman of *The Times* commented: 'Miss Bagnold holds a highly polished distorting glass up to life. So delicately adjusted, so witty, so graceful is the distortion that though we can take none of the characters in the glass quite seriously the attitudinisings are a joy to behold. They may not be true to life, but at least they are wonderfully true to the theatrical personalities of Dame Edith Evans, Miss Peggy Ashcroft and Mr Felix Aylmer . . .'

With *The Chalk Garden* successfully launched I began to think seriously of giving up my job as Edith's secretary. I had been with her for ten years, a long time to be with an overwhelming personality. I had not been a hundred per cent fit since the nervous breakdown, though I liked to think that I had still managed to help Edith, particularly through the *Nina* crisis.

So we agreed to part friends, and one evening we said goodbye at the junction of Sackville Street and Piccadilly, probably on the same spot where my nervous troubles had caught up with me. I watched Edith go on towards the Haymarket, then I turned up towards Regent Street and the bus for Gloucester Place.

Chapter Twenty-one

For the next five years my meetings with Edith were at infrequent intervals. She had her work, and her country home, but above all she had Judith, always on hand to deal with any emergency. The only job that I carried on, and was to do so for twenty years, was one which we called 'doing the Christmas cards'. This entailed consulting innumerable lists which I had kept over the years, and which only I could understand. The current secretary was only too pleased to leave me to it.

Edith's cries for help would arrive early in November and I would bustle off to Heal's and the Medici Gallery to beg the loan of their immense Christmas Card books to take back to Edith to choose her card, or sometimes I would go to the wholesalers in Albemarle Street and Soho Square. It was all very exhausting, but not nearly as exhausting as getting Edith to sit down and write in the cards. The whole business bored her to distraction but she insisted on writing a personal message in every card however many hundreds there were.

But if Edith was bored I enjoyed every minute of it; it was a chance to return, however briefly, to the life which I loved and missed so badly.

I should have been happy in my retired state, but I was not. I was well-off financially, thanks to my father from whom I had inherited a modest flair for the Stock Exchange, and in those days of no Capital Gains Tax every penny was an untaxed bonus. I could afford mink. At least twice a week I could take friends to the Royal Ballet at Covent Garden. There were first nights. My diary was full of engagements but it was not what I wanted. I felt as I had done at Eastbourne after my nervous breakdown, that humdrum existence with humdrum people was impossible.

Judith died in 1960, a tragically short while after she and Edith had moved to Gatehouse. After two operations she had returned to the country, and throughout the summer before her death Edith was with her continuously. Judith slipped quietly away in her exquisite bedroom overlooking the hop fields, and Edith lost a loving and undemanding friend.

Drama came unexpectedly after Judith's death. It could have been very nasty; as it was it was unpleasant enough – Judith's jewellery, which she had left to an old friend and not to Edith, could not be found. The house was searched; the police were called in. Edith was suspect, as was the secretary-nurse who had looked after Judith.

While all this was going on Aubrey Pyke and his wife Boosie, friends of Edith's, came for the weekend and slept in Judith's room, which like Edith's at the other end of the passage was en suite with dressing-room and bathroom. In the bedroom was an antique oak desk and Aubrey, a connoisseur of antiques, knowing that this particular style of desk usually had a secret drawer, felt around for the spring. He found it, the drawer sprang open and, need I say it, there were the jewels! A happy ending and a great relief to everyone, particularly to the suspects.

In 1959 Edith had played in the Centenary Season at Stratford-upon-Avon, when she had been involved in a serious car crash. She had gone over to Grimsby to appear at some school function, and on the way back the car in which she was travelling was in collision with a lorry and she was thrown out, suffering concussion and wrist and knee injuries. She was taken to hospital, but after one night insisted on returning to Stratford with her wrist in plaster. That night she appeared in *All's Well That Ends Well*. A courageous gesture, and at that time Edith was seventy-one.

Now in 1961 she returned to Stratford to play the Nurse in *Romeo and Juliet* and Queen Margaret in *Richard III*.

I have a gramophone recording of Act IV Scene iv of *Richard III*, where the rhythm of Edith's speech beats in the head like a musical score:

> *I had an Edward, till a Richard kill'd him;*
> *I had a Henry, till a Richard kill'd him:*
> *Thou hadst an Edward, till a Richard kill'd him.*
> *Thou hadst a Richard, till a Richard kill'd him.*

And again:

> *Where is thy husband now? where be thy brothers?*
> *Where be thy two sons? wherein dost thou joy?*
> *Who sues, and kneels, and says, God save the Queen?*
> *Where be the bending peers that flatter'd thee?*
> *Where be the thronging troops that follow'd thee?*

If I were asked which record I would take to a desert island, this would be my first choice.

Playing with Edith in *Richard III* was Esmé Church. I first met Miss Church in 1935 when she was playing with my friend Phyl Morris in *Mrs Nobby Clark*, directed by Murray Macdonald, at the Comedy Theatre. She was a true woman of the theatre as, apart from acting, she had in the days of Lilian Baylis been Head of the Old Vic School of Acting, and later Director of the Bradford Civic Theatre. It was while she was at the Old Vic in 1936 that she directed Edith as Rosalind and Michael Redgrave as Orlando in a memorable production of *As You Like It*, with lovely Watteau-esque costumes and settings by Molly McArthur.

Esmé Church was now cruelly crippled by arthritis but could still play old lady parts; she was playing the Duchess of York in *Richard III*.

I went down to Stratford to see the plays, travelling with Lucille Harris. Although many years Edith's junior, her understanding of her was remarkable. Also travelling with us was Edith Hargraves, another friend of Edith's who started as a 'fan', had been Michael Redgrave's secretary, and was Lynn Redgrave's godmother.

Lucille told us that Edith had to get rid of her latest secretary, a story which need not concern us here, but at once my thoughts turned to the fact that with Judith gone, and no secretary, Edith might need an arm to lean on.

I was right, but I did not become Edith's secretary. I never took that on again; my role was that of a kind of friend who could be be called upon when the need arose.

I stress 'a kind of friend', as Edith was eighteen years my senior. As I have said before, she had no great affection for me. What her feelings for me were I never knew, but unlike her married friends I was always available, particularly in troublous times.

Had I then read *Katherine Mansfield: The Memories of LM*, I would have better understood our relationship and been better able to cope. But unfortunately the book was not published until 1971 and this was 1961.

Many facets of Katherine Mansfield's character were analogous with Edith's. It could be Edith speaking when Katherine writes to LM: 'And whenever we do meet again let it be in freedom – don't do things for me! I have a horror of personal lack of freedom. I am a secretive creature to my last bones.' In the same way Edith was exasperated if I helped her out of a chair, or took her arm crossing the street.

And I might be speaking when LM writes: 'The unconscious feeling that I must always be "on call" for Katherine was so deep that I never thought of mentioning it to Susie [a friend].' Neither did I mention my 'on call' duties to my friends, which was the reason that I alienated so many of them.

In the Foreword to the book, Sylvia Berkman wrote: 'At points she was needed though not wanted . . . In each time of need it was she who was able to come, and who did come.' There must be hundreds of LMs and JBs who never learnt to play hard to catch.

But Edith and I got on well enough for long periods, and this was one of these periods. Of course I overdid it. When Edith asked me to the country I always accepted, thinking that she would be lonely on her own, and in the same way Edith asked me because she thought I was lonely in London. Actually there were times when we would both have preferred to be on our own, but it took time for us to sort this out. Had we been genuine friends such a situation could not have arisen. Edith would have said: 'I'd rather be alone this weekend', and I would have answered: 'So would I.'

But on the whole it was a happy time. There was a deep-freeze, a new toy which had to be filled with fruit and vegetables from the garden while Edith was in Dorset filming *Tom Jones*. The garden was large and a constant source of joy. I enjoyed gardening and got on well with William, who was even more important than Potter had been in Edith's life.

When Edith and Judith first went to Gatehouse, Judith advertised for a chauffeur-gardener. William, then a long distance coach driver with the Southdown Motor Company, answered the advertisement. His surname was Houghton, and being on the local council he was entitled to call himself Councillor Houghton, but his christian name was not William. I have no idea what it was; Judith and Edith christened him William as being a suitable name for a chauffeur.

William was a cockney who at some time had migrated to Kent and now lived with his wife and family in the village at the top of the hill. They were a remarkable family. One son was a successful architect, while Joan, who when still a schoolgirl came to Gatehouse to cook the most magnificent Sunday lunches for any number up to eight, later became a schoolteacher rising ever higher in her profession. Mrs Houghton, a small, indomitable woman, was just about perfect; her heart was pure gold.

William was a splendid driver with a wide knowledge of London streets and how to avoid the worst of the traffic, but of gardens, particularly flower gardens, he knew little. Judith was a knowledgeable gardener and William was anxious to learn; he was also devoted to Judith, as was everyone, and soon became extremely competent. When I was at Gatehouse he drove Edith to Coventry to take part in a Festival of the Arts in the cathedral, and while Edith stayed with Bishop Bardsley, William made a friend of the Bishop's head gardener who gave him chrysanthemum cuttings. This started William off on a passion for taking cuttings himself and doing other fiddling little seed jobs.

When Judith died William became yet more deeply involved in Gatehouse, and when Edith was alone he would sleep in the flat built on to the kitchen so that she need not fear intruders. It was wishful thinking on both their parts, as from where William slept he could not possibly have heard what went on in the house.

What made William so attractive was his tremendous zest for life and his enthusiasm for whatever he was doing. But it was fatal to say: 'Will you come in and mend a fuse when you've finished pricking out those seedlings?' For the seedlings could wait, and did, while William ran down the garden path to the fuse box. By the end of the day the garden was littered with implements, discarded in preference to fuses, loose tiles, or washers on the taps.

The trouble was that William could do so many things, from carrying logs the size of young trees into the hall and building a fire so fierce that strong men would move back into the shadows and take off their coats, to waging war on the squirrels who made a nest under the roof above Edith's bathroom using, in the process, every scrap of lagging off the pipes.

Of course he had his faults. He had a quick temper and could flare up without warning. Working for a conventional employer would not have appealed to him, and although he and Edith had rows they understood each other, perhaps because they were both cockneys.

It was an ideal job for William with his love of variety. He met interesting people, people whom he could watch on the television. He went to interesting places. He drove Edith to Buckingham Palace, to the Mansion House, to 10 Downing Street, and to the film studios and television centres. He enjoyed gossiping to the other chauffeurs while he waited, and he enjoyed driving the Rolls-Royce Silver Cloud: speaking from experience no one could have driven it better.

Both William and Mrs Houghton, who came to work at Gatehouse after retiring from her job at the village school, were wonderfully loyal to Edith and it is interesting to reflect that whereas Edith had secretaries and housekeepers galore, William remained; proof, if it were needed, that much friction and misunderstanding would have been averted had Edith had an all-male staff.

Chapter Twenty-two

Between November 1961 when the Stratford season closed, and November 1963 when Edith played in Robert Bolt's *Gentle Jack*, she took part in a number of poetry readings with Christopher Hassall. They got on well together, had the same sense of humour, and could share the same jokes. When he died suddenly, running to catch a train and collapsing in the railway carriage, Edith missed him sadly.

I often met Christopher Hassall at Gatehouse where he would come and stay the night so that he and Edith could discuss the poems for their next reading. He had recently gone to live at Tonford Manor near Canterbury, and was full of plans for its furnishing and restoration. He would usually arrive for the night with some old and very begrimed oil painting which he had just bought, and which he hoped when cleaned might prove to be an Old Master!

One of their readings was on a Sunday at the Chichester Festival Theatre when Edith invited me to go with them; as it was a lovely sunny day, I preferred to stay in the garden and weed the herbaceous borders. Another reading was at the Marlowe, Canterbury, where the date coincided with Edith's fiftieth year on the stage. This had not registered with her – dates were not important – and the hullabaloo, presents and telegrams, came as a complete surprise.

These readings, as I made clear earlier, did not inspire me with any great enthusiasm. I preferred reading poetry to myself. My father adored reading to us children, and would put on what we called his reading-aloud voice. Poetry readers often seem to put on a poetry voice, and to listen to them is purgatory for me.

I had always been disappointed with Edith's reading of non-Shakespearian verse until one evening at Gatehouse when Judith played some poetry recordings made by the BBC in 1945 when Edith was in India entertaining the troops. The poems were by Rabindranath Tagore. They were very beautiful and Edith spoke them so simply and sincerely that they really did bring a lump to the throat. They were a revelation of the art of speaking poetry. The BBC had given the recordings to Edith, and if they have their own copies they should look them out and play them for poetry lovers to admire and marvel.

It was a pity that there was no one close enough, or of sufficient standing, to insist to Edith that she only read poems which suited her individual style. When Dylan Thomas died in 1953 there was a Tribute to him at the Globe Theatre, and along with Richard Burton and Emlyn Williams, Edith read some of his poems. She was not suited to them and she did not really understand them. When I went to buy the gramophone record which was made at the Tribute, Edith's readings were not included. I was furious, but in my heart I knew the reason why.

It was at this Tribute that an officious woman brought Augustus John into Edith's dressing-room to introduce them. She gushingly informed Edith how much Augustus John wanted to meet her, although it was clear, as Edith said later, that he had no idea who she was and had probably never heard of her. But they were charmingly polite to each other, and both I and Phyl Morris, who was with me, had our evening made by meeting Augustus John in person.

After Christopher Hassall's death it was some time before Edith started reading again, this time on her own. Now she did read more satirical and humorous verse, and also developed a more intimate style which was very pleasing. Muriel Adams and I went to hear her at Fenton House in Hampstead and for the first time I really enjoyed hearing Edith read. But despite this, my opinion that she was not temperamentally suited to recital work, remained unshaken. She was first and foremost an actress who identified herself with the play and with her own characterisation within the play.

Edith did not share my opinion, which of course she never heard, and in 1973, at the age of eighty-five, she was still reading, this time in a programme entitled 'Edith Evans . . . and Friends', the friends being two young pianists, Antony Lindsay and Simon

Young. John Barber, drama critic of the *Daily Telegraph*, went down to Richmond to hear her, and wrote of her 'bejewelled Hardy Amies gown of the palest eau de nil', which showed that Edith continued to give her audience value for money. She never attended a function or appeared on a stage where she was not dressed impeccably and gloriously, putting to shame some of the over-dressed women appearing with her.

John Barber went on to say that 'every syllable she spoke, and every letter in each syllable, pealed out clarion-clear'. And he concluded: 'I very much hope that in the New Year Dame Edith will come to the West End with her friends, and her voice and her lovely gowns, and her impish humour.'

On 16 April 1974, Edith did come to the Haymarket Theatre in the West End. She came to rave notices, particularly in *The Times* and *Sunday Times*, and on the matinée day there was a queue of people outside the theatre waiting to buy seats. But I was disappointed; bitterly disappointed. The fact was that, despite the notices, Edith's voice, the voice her friends knew, particularly those who had known it in its prime, was now but a shadow of its former self. Where there had been authority there was now shrillness; every note was pitched an octave too high. A live recording had been made at the Richmond Theatre and I foolishly bought it to add to my collection of Edith records. Here the shrillness was even more apparent, it saddened me beyond words. My young friend in the record shop told me he thought it was wonderful; what he meant was that it was wonderful for an old woman. I played the record once or twice – then put it away.

Chapter Twenty-three

The visitors at Gatehouse were mostly Edith's 'chums', people whom she knew well and with whom she could relax and be at ease, and mostly they came for Sunday lunch, cooked by Joan. But some old friends like Muriel Adams, Edith Hargraves, and Boosie and Aubrey Pyke, who ran a superb catering establishment in Walton Street called Good Catering, would come for the weekend. Boosie and Aubrey eventually opted out when their catering skills spilled over into the weekend and they were called upon for so much advice and demonstration that the visits became too much like hard work.

Anyone thinking that theatre stars live in the lap of luxury should have come to Gatehouse. Certainly breakfast was taken in bed, but it was not brought to the bedside, instead each bedroom was provided with an electric kettle, and on retiring for the night we would mount the steep stairs (Muriel, who suffered from arthritis, almost on hands and knees) carrying a tray laid out with our breakfast requirements. Unfortunately there were no electric toasters so it was a case of bread or Energen rolls, but the idea was good in principle, and meant that people were not disturbed and could lie in bed as long as they wished.

Occasionally, very occasionally, people came who had to be provided with a cooked breakfast. When Peter Daubeny and his wife Molly came, there were bacon and eggs, and again when Edith's South African friends, Maisie and Harold Knox-Shaw and their son Peter, came to Gatehouse. I was shocked that Edith should get up and cook the breakfast, although I should have been more shocked had I been asked to cook it myself. I am sure that the people concerned had no idea that Edith was the cook, and imagined a posse of servants scurrying around in the kitchen. I should mention that this was the first time that Maisie came to Gatehouse; in the years ahead it would be she who cooked for Edith.

Edith often quoted a weekend when Judith entertained an elderly couple, friends of her mother's, when the catering continued non-stop – early morning tea, breakfast, mid-morning coffee, pre-luncheon drinks, luncheon, after-luncheon coffee, and so on to hot drinks at bedtime. It was what they were used to, but to Edith it was an outrage.

Why she felt as she did I cannot say, perhaps the old couple were rather boring and Edith never suffered bores gladly. Her own friends were never boring though they could be maddening, as was the case with Winifred who, though an expert gardener, pruned the branches of a rare and beautiful shrub which took years to grow a matter of inches. There must have been some chemicalisation between Edith and Winifred which brought out the worst in both of them, whereas when I went to film premières with Winifred I found her an amusing and stimulating companion.

American theatrical guests with their quick-fire wit were rather alarming, my preference being for the British who would discuss theatrical matters while I sat quiet, feeling – I am sure rightly – that they would resent my amateur opinions as Edith had done after my first nights. No such modesty inhibited Peter Knox-Shaw when, as a very young man, he came from Cambridge to stay at Gatehouse and constantly aired, what I considered his naïve opinions, while Edith and Peter Daubeny were discussing the World Theatre. I was scandalised and really angry, but as Edith and Peter Daubeny took it in good part it may have been that I just did not understand young men.

The guest I remember best was the film director Freddie Zinnemann who had directed Edith in *The Nun's Story*, and who came with his wife Renée, a much younger woman than Edith but extra ordinarily like her – tall, gay, altogether delightful, so that they could have been sisters. And I remember with affection Freddie Zinnemann pausing for a moment on the terrace in front of the house when he saw that I had brought out my camera.

Then there was Richard Church, poet and writer, with whom Edith shared a common childhood background of London in the

1890s, and with whom she loved to reminisce. I was always disappointed and surprised that the University of Kent never saw fit to honour with a doctorate this distinguished son and daughter of Kent by adoption.

Among other friends who came to Gatehouse were Margery and Geoffrey Castle who lived opposite Edith in Albany. Mrs Castle was Margery Sharp the novelist who, like G. B. Stern and Enid Bagnold was more interested in her plays than her novels. She had successfully adapted two of her novels, *The Nutmeg Tree* which starred Yvonne Arnaud, and *The Foolish Gentlewoman* which starred Sybil Thorndike.

Margery Castle would have liked to write Edith's biography, but Edith was violently opposed to the public being admitted to her private life. But even without this reservation she would not have chosen Mrs Castle. This was not a personal matter, she was extremely fond of the Castles, but at one time Mrs Castle, in her professional capacity as Margery Sharp, had given Edith advance copies of her children's books *The Rescuers*, and *Miss Bianca*. These were delightful books, concerned with a number of mice who, under the chairmanship of Miss Bianca, had formed a mouse Prisoners' Aid Society to rescue fellow-mice from the most terrible situations. The books compared favourably with Dodie's *One Hundred and One Dalmatians*, but to Edith they were whimsy, and whimsy was her pet aversion. The books lay on a table by the fire in Albany and Edith would moan: 'Why does Margery give me these mouse books?'

Among all these visitors to Gatehouse, there was one very important one indeed – Enid Bagnold. Enid Bagnold's husband, Sir Roderick Jones, Chairman of Reuters, died in 1962, and one day she rang to ask if she might come over from Rottingdean for lunch. Edith jumped to the conclusion that she wanted to share her grief with someone who had also lost a husband, and would therefore prefer to have Edith to herself. So as my mother was staying at the Spa Hotel in Tunbridge Wells I went there to have lunch.

When I returned and saw Enid Bagnold's car still in the drive, I decided to remain out of the way and, collecting my tools, went down to weed the rose garden. Some time later they came out on to the terrace and Edith introduced me. I never exchanged more than a few words with Edith Bagnold but I found her terrifying. I admired her unreservedly as a writer, but as a woman I was happy to keep my distance.

When she left Edith told me the truth of the matter. She had not come to weep but to bring the script of her latest play *The Chinese Prime Minister*.

Reading it that night I disliked it, so did Edith, so too did Muriel who came for the weekend. It had all the wordiness of *The Chalk Garden* without its wit and distinction. The proposition that Edith should play Mrs Forrest was politely shelved.

It may seem strange that after the disaster of *Nina* Muriel and I were still invited to read scripts. We were, but only just. Edith would never again allow our judgement to influence hers.

In the meantime Robert Bolt had written *Gentle Jack*. He said that he had written the part of Violet for Edith but the part was minuscule. Robert Bolt had a tremendous success with *Flowering Cherry* starring Celia Johnson and Ralph Richardson, which ran for 435 performances at the Haymarket Theatre, and an even greater success with *A Man for All Seasons* starring Paul Scofield, which when it was made into a film won many Oscars. *Gentle Jack*, however, was a dreary, muddled play of Hallowe'n rites and cloven hooves mixed up with big business, with Edith playing a female tycoon. She was not particularly interested, how could she be? But as with James Bridie and *Daphne*, she hoped that if she played Violet, Robert Bolt would then write her a bigger and better part. He never did.

The play, the production, everything about it, made so little impression on me that when I remember Edith's performances, I am apt to forget it. It opened at the Queen's Theatre in November 1963 and, as might have been expected, had only a short run.

Chapter Twenty-four

The speedy demise of *Gentle Jack* left Edith free in 1964 to play Judith Bliss in Noel Coward's *Hay Fever* for the National Theatre at the Old Vic.

When the idea was first mooted Edith was delighted and went to stay with Noel Coward at his home at Les Avants, near Montreux, where they discussed the play, in which Dame Marie Tempest had starred in 1925.

The question of age must have come up, but not alarmingly; it was only later that it assumed alarming proportions when considering the age of the rest of the company.

Louise Purnell and Derek Jacobi, who were to play Edith's children, were twenty-two and twenty-six respectively. Edith was seventy-six, though looking very much younger. The old man of the company, Anthony Nicholls, who played her husband, was fifty-seven, so even he was hardly in her age bracket, but at least they knew each other and had played together at Stratford in *All's Well That Ends Well*.

Noel Coward was to direct, and everyone knew his insistence on actors being word-perfect before rehearsals started.

This was not Edith's way: her way was to read the play several times, and what she called 'familiarise' herself with the part. I must have heard that word hundreds of times, and knew that it did not mean a thing. When Edith attended the first rehearsal she and the lines were total strangers, and it was not until she had walked the part that she would start to learn her words.

Of course she knew all about Noel's insistence on being word-perfect. It had been a thorny point between him and Gladys Cooper when she played in his *Relative Values* in 1951. On that occasion he made the remark to the effect that he did not expect Gladys to know all her words at the first rehearsal, but he had hoped she might know some of the words on the first night. But perhaps Edith preferred to ignore this story, or chose to relegate it to the back of her mind. Sufficient unto the day . . . And the day came at the first rehearsal when she was dismayed to find everyone word-perfect. They had to be. All except Edith were appearing in that year's repertory of plays and there was no time for fumbling about for words at rehearsals.

This made Edith feel insecure from the start. She felt she was holding them back. She probably was, and I imagine that rehearsals must have been grim.

It looked as if *Hay Fever* might be heading towards another *Nina*, though this time there was an accomplished cast and a brilliant director in Noel Coward.

Perhaps there was too much accomplishment, brilliance, and expertise, and I suspect too much ganging-up on Edith. Whatever the cause the wilting flower motif was back again. On the Sunday morning when we were due to start for the station *en route* for the opening in Manchester, it was plain that we were treading on quicksands. Then Gwen rang to ask if Edith would like her to come with us. I have never appreciated Gwen more than I did at that moment.

At the station everyone ignored us (Noel Coward was already in Manchester) and when Edith sent me to ask one of the company some questions about the time of the train, she took one look at me and walked away without answering.

The train had not travelled far before Edith was slumped in her corner as she had slumped in Olive's car on the way to Liverpool, and not long before she told us that it was impossible for her to play the part, and that Gwen or I must tell Noel that her understudy must go on.

It was a frightening admission, though not altogether a surprising one, and I was only too glad to leave Gwen to make soothing noises. There was nothing constructive to be done on the train, and nothing to be gained by argument, so we had lunch, though Edith ate nothing. On the way to the restaurant car I noticed the press representative and her husband playing cards with friends in an adjoining carriage, but no one had the courtesy to say hallo to Edith.

After lunch we sat in our carriage while the train wound its circuitous Sunday way over half the Midlands to get to Manchester. The only one to enjoy the journey was myself. It was a lovely day and the scenery was glorious, with the river Trent winding through fields with magnificent trees overhanging the banks. Then the train climbed slowly through hilly country, popping in and out of short tunnels, so that at one moment one was looking at mountain streams, then at sheep, then at stone cottages, then at rugged little railway stations not yet closed by Dr Beeching. It is as indelibly etched on my mind as the slate-grey drive from Liverpool to Essex.

For a reason which I have forgotten, perhaps because Edith wished to be on her own, she had arranged to stay at the Grand Hotel rather than the Midland (the Piccadilly was not then built), so as we drove away from the station we were further isolated from the rest of the company, who let us go without a word. It was obvious that these young people were antipathetic, indeed hostile to Edith; the reason was not clear unless something had happened at rehearsal of which I knew nothing.

When we reached the hotel there had been a mistake over the booking and there were no rooms for us. While I stood at the reception desk trying to sort things out, Edith sat in a chair, exhausted in mind and body. There was nothing I could do to conjure-up rooms; *Hay Fever* was to be an engagement in which everything went wrong, and so it was back into the taxi and a short drive to the Midland Hotel, where the management showed Edith to an almost pitch-dark room (it must have faced a well) which she refused to have. When at last she was settled in reasonable comfort she went to bed and Gwen went to the theatre to find Noel and tell him the worst. The thought of doing this, had Gwen not been there, still fills me with horror. My much simpler task was to ring Edith's Christian Science Practitioner and ask for help.

The next few hours were quite awful. Noel stormed up the corridor, followed by Gwen, and strode into Edith's room. I was left outside, but I could hear almost every word of the slanging-match which went on, so too could the few startled guests passing in the corridor. Noel accused Edith of being unprofessional, saying that no true professional would let a company down like this. He poured scorn on Christian Science for which he had a deep dislike since his one-time actress friend, Esmé Wynne Tyson (Stoj in his book *Present Indicative*), had taken to it in a big way. At one time I had known Esmé well and she always remained devoted to Noel. Now he accused Edith of being a poor advertisement for Christian Science.

It must be admitted that, to the casual observer, Edith was not a very good advertisement for Christian Science. Although the bathroom cupboard held no pills or medicine bottles, Edith was forced, from time to time, to resort to medical aid. But from a spiritual point of view her religion was all important; it was the bulwark against which she fashioned her life. To her, God was as real, and certainly more helpful, than any human friend.

But to return to Manchester. The outcome of all the unpleasantness was that Noel and Gwen forced Edith to attend the dress rehearsal that night. Gwen and I almost carried her out of the hotel and into a taxi. In the theatre I sat in her dressing-room with the script: the days were long past of being 'out by the half', and in fact I sat in the dressing-room every night for the next five nights, giving Edith what moral support I could and taking her through her words in the interval between each act.

I felt at the time that Noel hated the pair of us, and throughout this unhappy time Noel never spoke a word to me, and when I went into the passage to smoke a cigarette, not wishing to pollute Edith's dressing-room, he would pass by with a stony face and no look of recognition. He certainly never gave me credit for helping to get her on to the stage each night. The famous Coward charm was noticeable by its absence.

But I give him full credit for never having mentioned this difficult time in public, and speaking of Edith on television he said only the nicest things. He was a great professional, and as such did not wash professional dirty linen in public.

Gwen stayed for the first night for which I owe her a deep debt of gratitude. The afternoon before the opening she rested in my bedroom, having given up her own, and the many little bangles that she wore tinkled like temple bells as she slept peaceful as a child.

Someone else in Manchester was having an unhappy Coward-time. Cicely Courtneidge was appearing in *High Spirits*, a musical version of Noel's *Blithe Spirit*. Nothing was going right, but Cicely Courtneidge had a husband to give her moral support, and Jack Hulbert came to be with her. They sometimes sat next to us at supper after the performance, and Edith and Cicely Courtneidge would have a little moan together. How Edith envied her her husband.

Dame Cicely gave her own version of this time to Charles Castle for his book *Noel*, though I query her statement that Edith was 'in floods of tears'. I was with her at the time, and though she certainly looked as if she wanted to shed tears, I am sure she kept them back.

Here is part of what Dame Cicely said:

I'm a great admirer of Noel's, I have tremendous admiration for him. I think he's the cleverest man of our generation – a wonderful man, with great humour, but he's cruel. He's cruel as hell, and I'm no good when people are cruel to me. That's my only criticism of Noel. I don't think it's necessary to be like that, and when he was cruel to me I couldn't be funny on the stage any more. I can't work like that. I said to him, 'Noel, I want to go. I can't be funny. I'll never be funny again in this part.'

'One day,' I said, 'when you're not in the theatre, you come home and have a drink and I'll tell you why it's no good. Because you break people's hearts. You've got these wonderful ideas, and you're stubborn because you want it your way. You upset people, and I don't admire it.'

When we opened in Manchester, Edith Evans opened in the same week in *Hay Fever*. When my husband and I were lunching together, she used to come up to our table and say, 'Well, how are you getting on?' And she would be in floods of tears.

'Nothing will make me work for him again,' she cried. 'I've got enough money. I've got a home. Why should I be insulted?'

The awful Manchester engagement dragged to a close. One night Laurence Olivier came to see the play, and it was interesting to see the effect his charm had on Edith. Driving back to the Midland after the performance she literally blossomed like a rose, and was her old enchanting self again. He knew how to handle her, and his presence in Manchester throughout the run would have helped her immensely.

Edith could not get away from Manchester fast enough, and we travelled back to London on the night train on Friday. We had a carriage to ourselves and I put my feet up on the seat and fell asleep immediately. But Edith could not sleep and woke me from time to time to have a talk. The train arrived at Marylebone Station at five a.m. where Edith's good friend Lucille met us and drove us to our respective homes.

There was a day or two to go before the first night, and as Edith

On the terrace at Gatehouse (*l. to r.*), 'Boosie' Pyke, Dame Edith, the author, Lally Bowers

With Peter Daubeny (on the grass), his wife Molly, and Peter Knox-Shaw

Dame Edith in her cooking apron

'Shelling peas, aided by Edith Hargraves

was too nerve-ridden to sit in Albany, we spent the time tramping the streets.

Hay Fever opened on 27 October 1964. Edith gave an uncharacteristically unsure performance, which is borne out by the following two notices, though the critics did not realise why she was acting in the way she was.

First, Ronald Bryden in the *New Statesman*: 'I'm not sure about Dame Edith. She's not the Judith I imagine, though I can't think of anyone who'd make more of the evening than she does. Judith's surely, is a more purposeful idiocy, riper for that Lady Bracknell roar than for the vague swoopings and cooings with which Dame Edith dives from sofa to piano like a huge cuckoo.'

I remember those 'vague swoopings and cooings' and how they embarrassed me. I knew they were covering the fact that Edith was unsure of herself and did not really know her words.

Then there was the notice by the drama critic of *The Times*: 'The centrepiece of the evening, of course, is Edith Evans's Judith – a bold piece of casting – that magnificently justified itself. Dame Edith makes no attempt to present the Monstre sacré of the household as a middle-aged woman. She deliberately offers, and capitalises on, a ravaged appearance, stamping every line with comic authority, and wrathfully sweeping common sense aside whenever it challenges her moods of narcissism or outrageous romance.'

And why did Edith have 'a ravaged appearance'? Because she was so desperately nervous and unhappy that the ravaged appearance was, for the time at least, her natural appearance.

This was undoubtedly one of the most traumatic experiences of Edith's career. I have heard her say that if a doctor was in the wings on a first night, few actors, with their wildly thumping hearts, would be passed fit to go on.

Edith never attended first nights as a member of the audience; she was too aware of what her fellow actors were suffering, and she accused me of a lamentable lack of sensitivity in doing so. I was heartless; it was almost as bad as attending a public hanging. And I certainly never enjoyed one of Edith's first nights whilst it was in progress. I knew the play by heart, and when it came to a point where she had had difficulty learning the lines I would will her to clear the hurdle, while my head would sink lower and lower into my hands, much to the consternation of whoever I was with.

After the first night of *Hay Fever* Edith's performance gained in authority and in parts was brilliant, but it was never a happy engagement. At that time Maggie Smith was the darling of the Old Vic audience, but my opinion was that she over-acted as Myra Arundel, although the critics thought otherwise. Be that as it may, Edith found her difficult to play with.

Subsequently Celia Johnson took over the part of Judith Bliss, Edith being already committed to play Mrs Forrest in Enid Bagnold's *The Chinese Prime Minister*.

Chapter Twenty-five

Since we first read *The Chinese Prime Minister*, an improved version had been produced in New York in 1964 with Margaret Leighton playing Mrs Forrest. In the 1972 edition of *Who's Who in the Theatre*, the character is called She, which may be a mistake, but is more likely a literary tag attached to the name of Mrs Forrest.

We were told that the play had been a great success, which was not strictly true. It had played at the Royale, one of the smaller Broadway theatres, and had been a *succès d'estimè* rather than a commercial success.

Now Edith was to play Mrs Forrest, and Brian Aherne, after an absence from England of over thirty years, was to play her husband, Sir Gregory.

This was not a happy piece of casting. Brian Aherne may have been an excellent film actor, but on the stage he was uninspiring. Mrs Forrest had been an actress of note – one imagines that she was modelled on Dame Edith – and this man would have lighted no flame in her breast. Poor Brian Aherne knew he was miscast. It must have been a painful experience for him.

Vivian Matelon was the director. As I have said before, the only time I attended a rehearsal of one of Edith's plays was to see *Nina*, but one afternoon when I had something to deliver to the theatre where they were rehearsing *The Chinese Prime Minister*, Edith asked Vivian if I might stay for a while.

Watching this rehearsal gave me a new angle on Edith. The scene which I saw was one in which she was not sure of her approach. She went on and on about it. How should she play it? Where should she stand? What should she be doing?

When Murray Macdonald directed Edith and Owen Nares in 1937 in St John Ervine's *Robert's Wife* at the Globe Theatre, he told Dodie and me that Edith went on and on about the position of a cigarette box, which had to be moved before she could speak her lines. It was the same now, with the other actors standing around smoking cigarettes and reading newspapers, a look of infinite boredom on their faces. They must have felt like screaming, and it must have been particularly hard on those who had not worked with Edith before, perhaps had not even seen her act, and could not know that the finished product would be worth so much travail. It was not calculated selfishness on Edith's part, it was the penalty of being a perfectionist, but it could have been behaviour such as this which had alienated the young people in *Hay Fever*.

I never went with Edith to a film studio, but I am sure the same could not have happened there. Anyone who directed her in a film had a real love and admiration for her: Anthony Asquith, Freddie Zinnemann, and above all Bryan Forbes who directed her in *The Whisperers*, for which she won many awards.

The part of Mrs Forrest was extremely long and difficult to learn, having none of the wit and colour of Mrs St Maugham in *The Chalk Garden*. Enid Bagnold considered there was a plenitude of wit, an opinion which was to cause friction between herself and Edith during the production. She insisted that Edith was playing the part too seriously, but that was how Edith saw it and intended playing it.

There was no question of *The Chinese Prime Minister* developing into another *Nina* or *Hay Fever* tragedy. Mrs Forrest was a woman of mature age, Edith's age, but Edith was far from happy on the Sunday when we travelled to Cambridge for the opening at the Arts Theatre. We were booked in at the University Arms, an hotel which at that time was not interested in theatricals, nor willing to make allowances for difficult theatrical hours. If we were in for a meal we could have it, if we were late we could lump it.

We made a bad start by arriving too late for lunch. The 'we' included Alan Webb who had played the old butler Best in New York and was now playing him again. An old friend among the cast, though not staying at our hotel, was Peter Barkworth, playing Edith's son as he had done in *The Dark Is Light Enough*.

As there was no lunch we went to the theatre. As well as 'familiarising' herself with her part, Edith liked to familiarise herself with the theatre and her dressing-room. She was a workman getting to know her tools.

The Arts Theatre is tiny, seating about six hundred. Edith's dressing-room was also tiny, just a slip at the side of the stage. This tiny dressing-room played a part in Brian Aherne's violent antipathy to me.

Edith wanted me with her in the theatre, but there was no room for herself, her dresser, and me in the dressing-room. So I had to wander around, and the only place to sit was downstairs in an open space between the other dressing-rooms. I probably had no right to be there, but I was tired; there was a settee, and I sat on it. No one asked me to leave. And when Edith wanted to speak to me on the stage during the dress rehearsal I went to her. No one minded, or at least no one appeared to do so, except Brian Aherne.

I only assumed that he minded; like Noel Coward he never spoke to me, he just glared. But later at Brighton, where I was continually at the stage door, using the telephone to ring Edith's Christian Science Practitioner, I could hear him muttering to the stage-doorman: 'Why doesn't she go home? What does she think she's doing?'

I could have answered both questions, but I was there to help Edith, not to have a row with her leading man. I said nothing, either to him or to Edith, but it did not make life any easier. It must have been difficult for people who had not known me as Edith's secretary. Who was I? Was I her companion? I was not a friend, otherwise why did I call her Dame Edith? Very puzzling.

What made this engagement even more difficult was that for the first time in my experience Edith had a dresser with whom she was not *en rapport*. Joyce had not come into this category, she was devoted to Edith, she was just not temperamentally suited to be a dresser. But this dresser, though highly efficient, always remained withdrawn. Her attitude appeared to be – here's a star actress, she's bound to be difficult; well, I'm not going to be put on. But her assumptions were wrong. Edith wanted to be friends with her dresser, and she was not difficult, she was easy to dress; she had such a knowledge of clothes and how to wear them that there was little for her dresser to do but put her into the dress. Her needs in the dressing-room were small – a cup of coffee, a plate of grapes – but she did expect, or at least hope for, a cheerful face. In this instance her expectations were unfulfilled.

The first night at the Arts Theatre was better than might have been expected, but Enid Bagnold was not pleased. After the final curtain she came into Edith's dressing-room with her mouth set in a grim smile, the smile on the face of the tiger. 'How clever of you, darling,' she said, 'to invent so many new words for my play.'

It was a heartless remark to make to a sensitive actress who was exhausted after playing a long and difficult part. In Enid Bagnold's brilliant autobiography she writes with exasperation about Edith, and her reactions were probably sparked off by this unfortunate evening.

How different were Binkie Beaumont's reactions (he was presenting the play) as he left the theatre: 'Cherish her, Jean. Cherish her.'

This was to be the last time that Binkie presented Edith, although he would have presented her in 1971 in *Dear Antoine* had not her illness intervened.

Binkie died in 1973. To the general public he was barely a name, but to those who knew him in the thirty years of his heyday as a theatrical manager he *was* the West End theatre. I first met him when I was with Dodie. *Bonnet over the Windmill* was in rehearsal and I went down to Lilian Lawler who was designing the dresses to take some letters for Dodie's signature. In the salon I saw this unbelievably good-looking young man and wondered who he was. It was Binkie. He was presenting *Bonnet* as later he was to present *Dear Octopus*, and as he was to present Edith in almost every play in which she starred while I was with her. And in all that time he never appeared to change or grow a day older.

I shall always remember Binkie with affection as one of the few people who gave me credit for helping Edith, and I shall always remember his: 'Cherish her, Jean. Cherish her.'

Possibly Enid Bagnold was over-anxious that *The Chinese Prime Minister* should be a success. Her last play in London had been *The Last Joke*, produced in 1960, and despite the presence of John Gielgud and Ralph Richardson, had run for only 61 performances. It is only fair to say that when I saw it on the last night at the Queen's Theatre, I thought the critics had treated it unjustly.

134

So Enid Bagnold could not afford another flop and was looking to Edith to provide another *Chalk Garden*. But this time the material had not been provided.

I stayed in Cambridge until the middle of the week. I had never been there before, and I wanted to walk all over it and take it all in. I would have liked to visit Girton College. Professor Muriel Bradbrook, later Mistress of Girton, had been Judith's friend, and a friendship had developed with Edith. She stayed at Gatehouse one snowy New Year, and I remember her sitting on the floor in the hall before one of William's huge log fires, correcting the proofs of her latest book.

But there was no time for visits or sight-seeing, except one morning when Edith came out with me. Guy had been stationed at Caius for a time during the First World War, and Edith wanted to revisit it. But apart from this it was a repeat of our visit to the Manchester City Art Gallery. A glance at King's College Chapel, a whiff of the Backs, a hurried promenade up one street and down the next, then back to the hotel.

Gwen came to Cambridge to see the play and disliked it, and I picked it up again at Brighton, this time staying at the Royal Albion Hotel. Cathleen Nesbitt, of whom Edith was very fond, and who had seen the play in New York, came to a matinée and had a long talk with Edith in her dressing-room. She tried to persuade her to play the part lighter, and as Edith respected her judgement she did try, but continued to find more pathos than humour in Mrs Forrest.

I hated the first night at the Globe Theatre, where the play opened on 20 May 1965. And the notices the next day were bad. Here is an extract from *The Times*: 'Miss Bagnold falls into the trap of devoting too much attention to creating a star part and too little to the sense of the play. The part of Mrs Forrest supplies Dame Edith with ample material for characteristic displays of charm, capriciousness, age-defying vitality, and comic outrage . . . The part, indeed, plays so perfectly into her hands that it tempts her, most uncharacteristically, towards self-indulgence.'

Rather than accuse Edith of self-indulgence, I should say that she was indulging the author by trying too hard to find the plenitude of wit supposed to be buried in the play.

But some playwrights will continue to blame actors for the failure of their plays. Dodie did so on two occasions, when she should have blamed herself for the plays not being up to her usual standard. And when Edith played in a broadcast of Bernard Shaw's *The Millionairess*, Shaw rang Broadcasting House to say that the broadcast must be stopped immediately as Edith was ruining the part of Epifania and with it the play. The broadcast, which was going out live, was not stopped, and Shaw never forgave Edith. But as everyone knows, *The Millionairess* is not a good play.

Chapter Twenty-six

When *The Chinese Prime Minister* closed it was to be six years before Edith appeared in another play, although she did appear at the Mermaid Theatre in 1968 when she was the Female Narrator in Bernard Shaw's *The Adventures of the Black Girl in her Search for God*, but that was as a reader rather than as an actress.

This did not mean that Edith was idle. She made a number of broadcasts, and appeared on television, both in England where she played in BBC-2's two-part serial *The Gambler*, and in Canada and America where she played Lady Bracknell. She also took part in a Shakespeare reading in New York with John Gielgud and Margaret Leighton at the opening of the Lincoln Center World Fair Festival.

But it was filming which took up most of Edith's time, and from 1967 to 1970 she made five major films. In 1967 Edith made *The Whisperers*. Of this film Eric Shorter of the *Daily Telegraph* wrote: 'If Edith Evans does not get the prize for the best actress of the Berlin Film Festival this year, then the jury does not know fine acting when they see it.' And the film critic of the *Evening Standard* wrote: 'When they talk in years to come of how great an actress Edith Evans was, *The Whisperers* is the film they'll show to prove it.' In the same year Edith made *Prudence and the Pill*, a very bad film but one in which she wore some glorious modern dresses and walked unruffled across a race track with cars streaking past her at high speed.

The following year in *Crooks and Coronets* she played Lady Sophie

Fitzmore in a kind of modern version of the flying Duchess of Bedford, mixed up with a gang of crooks who took over her stately home. It was extremely funny, with an hilarious climax involving Clive Dunn and Hattie Jacques, but for some reason the critics murdered it. I saw it twice, the second time at Eastbourne, where the audience consisted of myself and one small boy. The small boy was convalescing from an illness, and feeling lonely in the empty cinema came to sit beside me; he was a nice little boy and enjoyed the film.

In 1969 Edith played Betsy Trotwood in the film of *David Copperfield*, with Robin Phillips as David. In 1970 she played in *Scrooge* which starred Albert Finney. She played one of the Christmases, past, present, or future, I cannot remember; it had little to do with Dickens.

While Edith was working her way through this remarkable record of work, I made an attempt to rescue my mother from hotel life which she detested. I gave up my London flat and took a flat at Eastbourne which we could share, but the operation was a complete failure; we had both lived on our own too long to join forces. After a year I returned to my old flat in Rossmore Court, fortunately empty again, and left Mother in possession of the Eastbourne flat.

While we were still trying to make a go of it, Edith came to stay. Mother was devoted to Edith who always showed her great affection, and on this occasion she cooked delicious meals while I carried on with entertaining Edith. At her request I took her to a Summer Show on the pier, where the compère welcomed the parties from the various boarding-houses, mentioning them all by name to terrific applause. I took her next to The Fol de Rols at the Congress Theatre, a highly professional entertainment of which Edith approved, and I also took her to the Theatre Royal, Brighton, to see Joyce Carey in *Heirs and Graces*, adapted from a novel by Ivy Compton-Burnett.

I worked hard entertaining Edith, too hard. She was not feeling well, a fact which she kept from me, and she had a nervous rash which itched intolerably and made her irritable. Had I known the reason for her irritability I could have made allowances, as it was I felt frustrated.

It had been arranged that we should return to Gatehouse together as William and Mrs Houghton were going on their summer holiday.

The arrangement was doomed from the start as we had already had more than enough of each other, or at least I had. So after a couple of days I invented an absurd story that Mother had rung and asked me to come home. Edith did not believe the story for a moment; how could she, knowing how unselfish Mother was? She was hurt. I had let her down and was leaving her alone in the house. It had happened before and was to happen again, but with anyone as forceful as Edith it was inevitable.

In J. M. Barrie's play *Dear Brutus*, one of the characters, Mr Purdie, says: 'It's not fate, Joanna. Fate is something outside us. What really plays the dickens with us is something in ourselves. Something that makes us us go on doing the same sort of fool things, however many chances we get.' And that was to be me, right up to the end.

A friend of Edith's, a witty and sophisticated woman of about her own age, once said that staying with Edith made her feel diminished mentally and physically. I knew what she meant. As the years passed, staying at Gatehouse became hard work, not that Edith asked anyone to do anything that she would not have done herself, but one could not sit back while one's hostess manhandled huge logs on to the fire, nor could one refuse to climb ladders and pick apples from the highest branches, knowing that a show of wavering would send Edith herself up the ladder.

Being alone with Edith at Gatehouse could be really frightening, and once almost ended in tragedy. The accident happened in the garden-room which had a low window-seat from which one could step out of the windows on to a mounting block and from there on to the terrace. It was an operation which needed a certain amount of balance and Edith should not have attempted it without someone to give her a hand.

But Edith disliked being given a hand or helped in any way, and on this particular Sunday afternoon, while I was washing-up in the pantry, I heard a cry, and running into the garden-room found Edith on the floor with blood pouring from her head. She had come in from the garden, slipped on the window-seat, and in falling had given her head a frightful crack against the wall.

Fortunately I was not alone. Lucille had arrived on cue from her country home nearby, and together we helped Edith on to her feet and into the downstairs cloakroom. I wanted to call a doctor, but she stopped me, telling me that I was panicking, as indeed I was, and that we should get on with bathing her head which was a mass of blood. Being a Christian Science home there were no medical supplies, but we did find a bandage in a kitchen drawer, and when the blood ceased to flow we bandaged her up, or at least Lucille did. Throughout the proceedings, although Edith must have been in great pain, she never lost her sense of humour, adapting Shakespeare to – 'Who would have thought the old woman to have had so much blood in her.' Not only blood but courage, and by the next morning the wound had almost healed.

It was not only blood with which one had to contend at Gatehouse; there was the kitchen. Joan was now a fully qualified school-teacher and there was no one to cook the Sunday lunch, or any other lunch, and the kitchen became a place to by-pass if possible. Edith was a first-class cook, rising to cordon bleu heights with certain dishes, but being an actress she needed an audience, and friends (not myself, the garden was accepted as my province) were required to prop up the sink as a one-man audience while Edith played her part. It was a small thing to ask but could become extremely tedious. A well-known actress who spent the night at Gatehouse, when asked by a friend to describe the garden, answered that she never saw it as she spent the morning in the kitchen.

Of course the meals were delicious, but most of us would have been content with lighter, more feminine meals. But Edith called these 'bachelor girl meals' and scorned them accordingly.

The fact was that it was difficult to live up to Edith with her quick wit and lightning intuition. She expected us all to be as quick off the mark as she was, and by the evening we were exhausted. I am speaking now of old friends whom Edith considered should be treated as one of the family. This was meant as a compliment, but if Edith was feeling out of humour the family atmosphere was strained to the limit.

So why did we come, and come again? I will tell you. I recall an afternoon when Maisie, Muriel and I were walking in the garden. Mrs Davies, Edith's splendid little Albany housekeeper, had given Maisie some alarming facts which pointed to the possibility that Edith might be ill. We were all appalled, and agreed unanimously that a world without Edith would be unthinkable. Edith at her best made up a hundredfold for Edith at her worst.

And Edith was at her best when she came again to Eastbourne in 1969. Mother, at ninety-two, had suffered a stroke and was in a nursing home. Edith came with me to visit her, being as charming as only she could, and giving Mother great pleasure. We also went bathing together. I hesitate to call it swimming as I had a strong suspicion that Edith kept a toe on the ground, but if so, at eighty-one she had a perfect right to do so, and she thoroughly enjoyed herself.

Chapter Twenty-seven

Dear Antoine came to Edith in 1971 via Sir John Clements and the Chichester Festival Theatre. It was a play by Jean Anouilh, and was to be directed by Robin Phillips, a happy association, as during the filming of *David Copperfield* he and Edith had formed a friendship of mutual affection and respect for each other's work.

Edith was to play Carlotta, an old woman. It was a good part and not too long. It would be in the repertory of the Festival so Edith would not be playing every night and could go home for weekends, and sometimes during the week. It sounded a perfect engagement.

What we did not know at the time, although Robin Phillips told me later, was that people in the theatre were saying that Edith had been too long away from the theatre; that at her age it would prove too tiring; that it was better for her to continue to concentrate on films.

When opinions like these are bandied about, although they may never reach the ears of the subject, they form an atmosphere and create their own results. In the same way, Dodie would never discuss the plot of a new play, not even with Alec. Her theory was that once one voiced an idea it somehow found its way into the air and other playwrights got the message, then several plays on the same subject would turn up at the same time. It did happen.

Rehearsals began in London, but as soon as the Festival opened they moved to Chichester. *Dear Antoine* was to be the second play in the repertory.

The Festival Theatre had accommodation for its players in the town and there were also the hotels. Edith had other ideas, and Lucille had driven her round the district to inspect various places; eventually she chose to stay in a private house at Itchenor, seven miles outside Chichester. The house was called Spinney House and belonged to a woman, recently widowed, who hoped by taking as a paying guest someone from the theatre during the Festival, to tide herself over until her husband's affairs were settled.

I had finally given up my flat in Rossmore Court and was now permanently settled at Eastbourne, not in the flat I had shared with Mother, but six floors up with a balcony overlooking the sea. On this balcony I grew flowers and trained ivy, later shedding tears of frustration when the winter gales tore everything to shreds. From here I went over to Gatehouse at weekends to hear Edith's words, and on Sunday night William would drop me at Lewes station when he drove Edith back in the Rolls to Itchenor.

But one weekend when Edith could not get home I went to Spinney House. I loved it. The house was a glorious open-plan affair, one of the most attractive houses I ever saw. There was an enormous sitting-room-cum-dining-room with windows on three sides, one set of windows folding back like shutters. Sitting there in the evening one looked out on a child's picture-book garden, with squirrels clambering up and down the trees, pheasants coming to be fed at the back-door, and the family cat watching over all with apparent approval. And that was not all. The garden, which was large, ran down to a tidal basin crowded with boats of all sizes and all colour of sail. At the weekend there was racing. It was paradise.

The furnishings of the house were mostly in teak, and every bedroom had its bathroom. The property would have fitted well between the covers of a glossy magazine.

I got on well with Agnes, our landlady, after recovering from the shock of her taking me for Edith's paid companion. Did I look like a companion? or was it that I was so much younger than Edith and called her Dame Edith? Perhaps Noel Coward and Brian Aherne had also taken me for a companion. If so it explained a great deal.

Unfortunately Agnes and Edith did not get on well; they were temperamentally incompatible. I suspect that Edith was a disappointment to Agnes who had expected an actress to be amusing, easy-going, fun to be with. But this actress was absorbed in her work with no time for frivolous chit-chat. Edith herself was not blameless, making no allowances for someone who knew nothing of the theatre, and people who know nothing of the theatre almost always say the wrong thing without realising it.

All this made for a strained relationship, when what Edith needed was complete harmony. It was a pity. It was also a pity that Edith had to drive seven miles to rehearsal and seven miles back. Had she stayed in an hotel in Chichester she could have sneaked the odd rest during the afternoon; as it was she was away from nine o'clock in the morning until seven o'clock at night, coming back exhausted.

She should have refused to work such long hours. Dame Marie Tempest, of whom I saw a great deal when she was playing in Dodie's *Dear Octopus*, always refused to rehearse in the afternoon and no one murmured; it would have made no difference if they had. Edith should have done the same, and Robin Phillips, a charming and sensitive young man, would have respected her wishes. But he was not a mind-reader, and it was difficult for a young man of twenty-nine to think himself into the mental and physical state of a woman of over eighty.

It may sound laughable to say that Edith did not assert herself sufficiently, but it was so. If her fellow-actors rehearsed all day so did she; it never occurred to her to ask for preferential treatment.

When I came down this first weekend I was distressed to see Edith looking so tired and worn. The trouble was not with learning her words; although she insisted on going over them time and time again, she was far more accurate than was usual at this stage. But she was sadly colourless and withdrawn, and would sit at table never speaking a word. On Sunday, Agnes's son, and her brother, came to lunch, two personable males who in the usual way would have brought out the best in Edith, but it was impossible to draw her into the conversation.

I was always proud of being associated with Edith, I still boast of it, and liked to watch her 'doing her stuff' and charming people as only she could. But now these men would go away saying: 'What's all this fuss about Edith Evans? She may have been a great actress in the past but she doesn't look like one now.'

Later when Agnes said to me that she thought Edith was too old and tired to play the part, and would never get on the stage, I replied that Edith was always like this when she was studying a part, and everything would be all right on the night. I should have remembered having said the same to Judith over *Nina*.

But Carlotta was not Nina. Edith was not too old for the part, and anyway the part was not a long one and she knew her words. She had no great burden of responsibility, it was shared by a company of distinguished players headed by Sir John Clements. I could see no reason for anything going wrong; her tiredness would vanish as soon as the play was produced. There was nothing to fear.

The next weekend we were back at Gatehouse. After that I did not see Edith for a while, although I rang her at Spinney House every night as she liked to have a talk. I had no idea how bad things had become until one Sunday morning, when I was breakfasting in bed and looking forward to a quiet day, the telephone rang. It was Edith. Would I come to Spinney House at once?

Even then I was not unduly worried. Perhaps she wanted a run through of words, and thinking I would be away for only a night or two I threw a few things into a bag, and leaving the washing-up and the unmade bed, rang for a taxi and just caught the train for Brighton where I had to change for Chichester.

The journey to Chichester should have taken about two hours; as it was it took almost five. The usual Sunday work was being done in a tunnel, and at Worthing we were turned out of the train and taken by bus to an obscure little station set down in the middle of fields, where we sat for two hours until a train was found to take us the rest of the way to Chichester. When I ultimately finished my journey by taxi there was a white-faced Edith looking out of the window, watching for me.

She was in a terrible state of nerves, but as we sat together while I ate the lunch that Agnes had kept hot for me, she relaxed a little. We went over the words, which she knew perfectly, and as there was a preview that night of *Dear Antoine*, I went with her to the theatre and sat with her in her dressing-room.

There were three previews in all, all of which I spent in Edith's dressing-room. My only relaxation was when she was on the stage and I could go down to the bar in the front of the house and take a glass of wine out on to the terrace. Most of the back-stage staff did the same, and as it was glorious May weather, with the trees and parkland surrounding the theatre looking wonderfully fresh and peaceful, I too dared to feel peaceful. Edith was getting through the previews without a hitch, and I thought 'she's going to make it'.

And she did make the first night which was a great success, and a personal triumph for Edith. After the final curtain her dressing-room was packed with admirers, including Margaret Leighton, dabbing her eyes, and telling Edith she had moved her to tears.

Driving back to Spinney House I was sure that our troubles were over. With the first night behind us everything would return to normal.

I could not have been more mistaken. The next morning Edith was utterly exhausted. She had keyed herself up for the first night; there was nothing left.

It was now that Edith propounded a piece of illogical reasoning, which to her was completely logical, and which must have been in her mind from the start of rehearsals. It was, that now she had 'given Robin his first night', she had done her bit. She kept on repeating: 'I've given him his first night, he's got his notices, no one can take them from him.'

Robin had certainly received good notices for his production, but had he not done so I doubt whether it would have altered Edith's attitude. She had put a limit on her powers of endurance and further than that she could not go. She had reached what she had always considered as the finishing line, and having won the race no one had a right to expect her to go on running. She was too exhausted, mentally and physically, to consider what effect her withdrawal would have on the production or on the rest of the company.

It was a thousand pities, for everyone in the company loved and admired her, particularly the young people. I heard them say how much they had learnt watching her in rehearsal, and they treated her like a queen. Edith's little dresser wore neither shoes nor stockings, but was a wonderful support both to Edith and myself. Edith said she was the best dresser she had ever had.

And then there was Robin Phillips, who despite every upset gave Edith unfailing loyalty and affection. There was one actress who had a scene where she sat beside Edith on a bench, and Robin said: 'What ever you do, don't act, it looks dreadful. You're sitting next to someone who doesn't act, she *is*!'

But none of this good-will could help Edith now. She played the next night, but only just; it was all her dresser and I could do to get her on to the stage. As so often in the past I was continually ringing her Christian Science Practitioner, who must have been as worn out as I was. That night I needed my glass of wine more than ever.

The following morning I had to ring Olive Harding, who was fortunately staying with friends near by, and after coming over and seeing Edith she rang the theatre to say that Edith could not go on that night. This meant a doctor and a certificate. The doctor was a charming man who produced bottles of sedatives and said that Edith must rest for a few days. It had all happened before in Liverpool in 1955.

The next morning, a Saturday, William fetched us and we drove home to Gatehouse.

Our respite was short-lived. On Sunday night Sir John Clements rang to say that Binkie Beaumont was coming to see the play with the idea of presenting it in London after the Festival. Would Edith please come.

Edith agreed to come, but she had already made up her mind to leave the company. Once again Olive was contacted, and it was arranged that she should be at the theatre the following afternoon. Olive was a remarkable woman, a magnificent agent, and a good friend to Edith.

On Monday we were back on the now familiar road to Chichester. When we arrived Olive and her friend Joyce were waiting, and while Joyce and I sat in the car the others went into the administrative building for a conference with Sir John who was determined that Edith should stay.

The conference dragged on for hours. At one point Sir John, looking remarkably grim, went across to the theatre to tell the stage manager that Edith's understudy must go on. People were arriving for the evening performance, and I thought of their bitter disappointment on hearing that Edith was not playing. But by this time she had been persuaded, or should one say bullied, into not leaving the company but rejoining it the following night.

Did Edith remember Cicely Courtneidge and how Jack Hulbert had come to be with her in Manchester? Did she feel very much alone? Of course there was Olive, but agents are pulled two ways. They cannot afford to alienate managements on whom depends the livelihood of their clients, the actors. Life for Olive was a perpetual see-saw on which she had to try and keep a balance.

So for the time being Edith was to stay, but she preferred not to return to Itchenor. She had had enough of driving back and forth along that road, so William and I drove there, and having paid the bill we packed up and returned to the Ship Hotel in Chichester which had a vacant room with a private bath.

As I had expected to return to Gatehouse that night I had not brought my inadequate little hold-all, not even a tooth-brush, so Olive and Joyce offered to stay with Edith while I went back with Willam. I promised to return the following morning.

Oh, the joy of being free for even a few hours! William took off his chauffeur's cap, and together we sped back along the road. Mrs Houghton was waiting for us and cooked my supper, while I washed some clothes which sorely needed it. Then I sent the Houghtons home, though they offered to stay, and I was alone for the first time in days.

The following morning we were back at the Ship Hotel and I could see that Edith's state, far from improving had worsened. She looked ghastly, and the innumerable pills, to which she was un-accustomed, had a doping effect, so that when she insisted on going for a walk she stumbled in the road and almost fell. I steered her back to the hotel and into the restaurant for lunch, but she hardly knew where she was. Eventually I got her to bed. There was no question of her playing that night, instead she said she would play the matinée next day.

I was certain she never would. Each time she postponed the dreaded moment of going on the stage the relief brought an upsurge of well-being, but as time ran out the ill effects returned, worse than before. I knew that it would continue like this until Edith was allowed to quit.

It became more and more difficult for me to cope. At one time I had to fetch Robin Phillips from the theatre in the middle of the evening so that Edith could go over with him the same old story of having given him his notices, and how it was not important for her to be there any more.

He was infinitely patient, but as he was leaving he asked me: 'Do you think she will ever go on?' and I answered: 'Never. The only thing is to let her go.'

Looking back after the event, after the heart-attack which nearly killed her, and from which she made such a miraculous recovery, one realises that Edith was a very sick woman, not just a nerve-ridden one. Knowing this, could I have carried on? I think not.

She had become increasingly irascible. When I first went to Spinney House she had repeatedly said: 'I'll never forget what you've done for me; if there is ever anything I can do for you,' etc. But now whatever I did was wrong.

The doctor told me that I was doing her no good, that she took me too much for granted. He was giving me a loop-hole through which to escape. I allowed myself to believe that I had outstayed my usefulness. It was what I wanted to believe. I had already had one nervous breakdown, the effects of which had lasted for years, but from which I was now free. The thought of having another was more than I could bear.

What added to my feeling of strain was that Edith's close friends were either too old, or in the case of Lucille too occupied with her family, to come to my assistance. If Edith left the company, now almost a certainty, and if I returned with her to Gatehouse, I risked being tied to her chariot wheels for the rest of my life.

I remembered that years before, in 1950, I had seen *Ring round the Moon*, a play by Christopher Fry from the French of Jean Anouilh. One of the characters, played by Dame Margaret Rutherford, was a demanding and cantankerous old woman in a wheel-chair, who had a companion whom she bullied unmercifully. At the time I took this as a warning (perhaps I was in an anti-Edith mood), saying to my-self: 'Oh no! You must never let that happen to you.' Was it about to happen?

I was letting my imagination run away with me, but I had lived with *Dear Antoine* for over six weeks, and for the last two weeks had lived out of a small hold-all containing one dress and a far too warm Hanro suit, with either of which I had to wear a pair of old sandals, having cut my foot before leaving. As to the flat, the bed was still unmade, the dirty dishes still on the draining-board, the letters and newspapers still piling up on the floor. Being tidy-minded, I was distressed.

Worse than this, I had not even had the satisfaction of seeing *Dear Antoine*. On one of the five nights when Edith was playing I plucked up courage to ask Sir John if I might stand at the back, but he told me rather crossly that the fire regulations made it impossible. Carlotta was only the second of Edith's parts in forty years which I

149

never saw. The first had been Helen Lancaster in *Waters of the Moon* when I had my nervous breakdown. Now Edith was having the breakdown, and worse.

Now the curtain was coming down on more than just a play. It had finally been decided that Edith should leave the cast, and Olive and Joyce, who had gone home to Dorset, returned to Chichester. When I told them that I could no longer carry on but must go home, they agreed. By then I was probably looking fairly ill myself. Olive would see to the business of Edith's withdrawal from the company, while Joyce would do her packing. William was already on his way to drive her home.

When I went into Edith's room to say goodbye, she said: 'Aren't you going to kiss me?' an absolutely unheard of request as we never kissed. I gave her a peck on the cheek and she said: 'Please get in touch with me when you have got over all this.'

As I handed in my keys at the reception desk the manageress looked at me in astonishment, saying: 'Surely you're not going to leave Dame Edith alone?' 'She's not alone,' I blustered, 'Miss Harding and her friend are with her.' But I could see that my lame excuse had not reached a sympathetic ear. How could it? But I genuinely believed that once Edith was home, freed from *Dear Antoine* as she had been freed from *Nina*, she would recover quickly. I was wrong, and Edith never forgave me for letting her down.

Sitting on a seat on Chichester railway station, waiting for my train, I was already regretting my decision. How many times, in imagination, have I sat on that seat and then returned to the hotel. Prisons must be full of prisoners regretting that they did not follow the dictates of their conscience, but like those same prisoners I continued on my way, a decision which, however often I dream to the contrary, can never be reversed.

Arriving back in Eastbourne I was so relieved to be home, and so exhausted, that I could not face the thought of ringing Edith and perhaps being recalled to duty. Instead I bathed in the sea, regained my strength, and it was July before I at last wrote to Edith. It was too late, and she would not see, speak, or write to me.

She was just starting her long heart illness, but that I did not know. The first I heard of it was months later when a friend of hers wrote to say that he was helping to move her things from Albany to the country, and what did I want done with a folding bed I had lent her. He also returned a pair of silver grape scissors which I had once given to Edith.

I wrote to thank him, enclosing a postal order for the postage on the scissors – a childish gesture but I was deeply hurt. A pair of grape scissors! Every time I use those scissors, and I use them daily, I am reminded of *Dear Antoine* and of Barrie's words: 'What really plays the dickens with us is something in ourselves. Something that makes us go on doing the same sort of fool things, however many chances we get.'

What Barrie did not say, though he must have known it, was that there comes a day when our chances run out. Mine ran out on Chichester railway station at 10.20 on the morning of Thursday 27 May 1971.

Epilogue

And now Edith is dead. I heard of her death on Thursday 14 October 1976 on the two o'clock Radio News Summary. It was not a time when I usually listen but, for some unknown reason, I switched on. A few minutes later Mrs Houghton rang; she had promised to do so if anything should happen to Edith, and in her kindly, thoughtful fashion, she kept her promise.

The end had been peaceful. Edith had a cold and went to bed. Later she wished to change from her large and rather austere room into what was called the Blue Room where I, and others of her friends, had so often slept. It was a charming, cosy place of glazed chintz curtains and covers. William helped her to move. Half-an-hour later she died.

After the radio came the television tributes; how Edith would have hated them with their insistence on Lady Bracknell and that handbag, but the tribute on that night's radio edition of Kaleidoscope was one that would have had her unreserved approval. It was presented by John Powell with a moving personal tribute from Michael Elliott.

The end of an era; for me the end of hoping. Every morning since that dreadful débâcle at Chichester in 1971, I had woken with the hope that a letter would drop on to the carpet; that the telephone would ring; that Edith would relent and say: 'Come and see me.' It was hard to abandon hope for ever.

What thoughts passed through my mind? Two to do with death. Edith sitting by the fire at Gatehouse and saying, perhaps half joking: 'If I live to be very old, how will Guy and Mother and Father recognise me?' And later: 'I should like a memorial plaque in St Paul's, Covent Garden, to Mother and Father, Guy and myself.'

How do I remember Edith in a personal, private way? Opening the door to me in Albany in her brown and white checked Molyneux suit. A day in 1947 when I drove Chloe along a straight stretch of the London to Eastbourne road with not another car in sight, the speedometer teetering between seventy and eighty, and Edith roused from her cat-nap: 'Not so fast, Jean.' Edith coming with me to see mother in the nursing home, and mother's pride and joy, and her delight in telling the nurses: 'That was Dame Edith Evans.' Edith in the kitchen at Gatehouse, sitting on the high stool in the corner, wearing the red and white cooking apron I bought her at Harrods. And Edith in the garden at Gatehouse with Freddie and Renée Zinnemann; with Maisie and Harold Knox-Shaw; with Molly and Peter Daubeny.

And then there is the theatre. The second night of *Daphne Laureola* with Queen Mary in the royal box, and Murray Macdonald, Johnnie Stevens and myself standing at the back of a Packed Dress Circle, watching Edith give one of the greatest performances of her career in the part of Lady Pitts.

Moving back into the theatre of the thirties, there I am, night after night, standing at the back of the pit to watch Edith play Rosalind to Michael Redgrave's Orlando, or standing at the back of the gallery to watch Edith play Sanchia Carson in St John Ervine's *Robert's Wife*.

Edith, who could be wonderful or maddening; a woman without natural beauty, but one who could transform herself into a ravishing charmer. It is not for me, an amateur, to assess her acting, I cannot do better than quote a great actor on a great actress. Here is the final paragraph of Sir John Gielgud's appreciation of Edith, printed in the *Observer* on Sunday 17 October 1976:

Supreme mistress of high comedy and farce, a brilliant and versatile character actress rich in power and emotional conviction, the name of Edith Evans must surely rank with the greatest of her sisters in the history of our theatre – the Abingdons and Bracegirdles, Madge Kendal, Marie Tempest and Ellen Terry.

Index

158